06/02

ARETHA
FRANKLIN

ARETHA FRANKLIN

Jim McAvoy

CHELSEA HOUSE PUBLISHERS
Philadelphia

Dedicated to Mom, Dad, Don, Mike, Connie, Dan, Joe, Megan, Mary Katherine, and Joseph Frederick—the most important people in my life.
In memory of Constance Harris.

Chelsea House Publishers

Editor in Chief	Sally Cheney
Associate Editor in Chief	Kim Shinners
Production Manager	Pamela Loos
Art Director	Sara Davis
Director of Photography	Judy L. Hasday
Cover Designer	Takeshi Takahashi

The Chelsea House World Wide Web address is
http://www.chelseahouse.com

First Printing 1 3 5 7 9 8 6 4 2

Library of Congress Cataloging-in-Publication Data

McAvoy, Jim.
  Aretha Franklin / Jim McAvoy.
    p. cm.—(Black Americans of achievement series)
  Includes bibliographical references and index.
  ISBN 0-7910-5808-5 (alk. paper)—SBN 0-7910-5809-3 (pbk.: alk. paper)
   1. Franklin, Aretha—Juvenile literature. 2. Soul musicians—United
States—Bibliography—Juvenile literature. [1. Franklin, Aretha. 2. Singers. 3. Soul music.
4. Afro-Americans—Biography. 5. Women—Biography.] I. Title. II. Black Americans of
achievement.

ML3930.F68 M33 2000
782.421644'092—dc21
[B]
                                                                    00-060134

Frontispiece: Aretha Franklin, the Queen of Soul, brings her powerful voice and commanding presence to every performance.

CONTENTS

On Achievement 8
Coretta Scott King

1
A Rose Is Still a Rose 11

2
Life in the Church 17

3
The Columbia Years 27

4
R-E-S-P-E-C-T 37

5
Amazing Grace 47

6
Changes 57

7
The Road Back 69

8
What You See Is What You Sweat 81

9
The Reign Continues 91

Chronology 102

Selected Discography 104

Grammy Awards 106

Further Reading 107

Index 108

BLACK AMERICANS OF ACHIEVEMENT

HENRY AARON
baseball great

KAREEM ABDUL-JABBAR
basketball great

MUHAMMAD ALI
heavyweight champion

RICHARD ALLEN
religious leader and social activist

MAYA ANGELOU
author

LOUIS ARMSTRONG
musician

ARTHUR ASHE
tennis great

JOSEPHINE BAKER
entertainer

JAMES BALDWIN
author

TYRA BANKS
model

BENJAMIN BANNEKER
scientist and mathematician

COUNT BASIE
bandleader and composer

ANGELA BASSETT
actress

ROMARE BEARDEN
artist

HALLE BERRY
actress

MARY MCLEOD BETHUNE
educator

GEORGE WASHINGTON
CARVER
botanist

JOHNNIE COCHRAN
lawyer

BILL COSBY
entertainer

MILES DAVIS
musician

FREDERICK DOUGLASS
abolitionist editor

CHARLES DREW
physician

W. E. B. DU BOIS
scholar and activist

PAUL LAURENCE DUNBAR
poet

DUKE ELLINGTON
bandleader and composer

RALPH ELLISON
author

JULIUS ERVING
basketball great

LOUIS FARRAKHAN
political activist

ELLA FITZGERALD
singer

ARETHA FRANKLIN
entertainer

MORGAN FREEMAN
actor

MARCUS GARVEY
black nationalist leader

JOSH GIBSON
baseball great

WHOOPI GOLDBERG
entertainer

CUBA GOODING JR.
actor

ALEX HALEY
author

PRINCE HALL
social reformer

JIMI HENDRIX
musician

MATTHEW HENSON
explorer

GREGORY HINES
performer

BILLIE HOLIDAY
singer

LENA HORNE
entertainer

WHITNEY HOUSTON
singer and actress

LANGSTON HUGHES
poet

JANET JACKSON
musician

JESSE JACKSON
civil-rights leader and politician

MICHAEL JACKSON
entertainer

SAMUEL L. JACKSON
actor

T. D. JAKES
religious leader

JACK JOHNSON
heavyweight champion

MAGIC JOHNSON
basketball great

SCOTT JOPLIN
composer

BARBARA JORDAN
politician

MICHAEL JORDAN
basketball great

CORETTA SCOTT KING
civil-rights leader

MARTIN LUTHER KING, JR.
civil-rights leader

LEWIS LATIMER
scientist

SPIKE LEE
filmmaker

CARL LEWIS
champion athlete

JOE LOUIS
heavyweight champion

RONALD MCNAIR
astronaut

MALCOLM X
militant black leader

BOB MARLEY
musician

THURGOOD MARSHALL
Supreme Court justice

TERRY MCMILLAN
author

TONI MORRISON
author

ELIJAH MUHAMMAD
religious leader

EDDIE MURPHY
entertainer

JESSE OWENS
champion athlete

SATCHEL PAIGE
baseball great

CHARLIE PARKER
musician

ROSA PARKS
civil-rights leader

COLIN POWELL
military leader

PAUL ROBESON
singer and actor

JACKIE ROBINSON
baseball great

CHRIS ROCK
comedian and actor

DIANA ROSS
entertainer

WILL SMITH
actor

WESLEY SNIPES
actor

CLARENCE THOMAS
Supreme Court justice

SOJOURNER TRUTH
antislavery activist

HARRIET TUBMAN
antislavery activist

NAT TURNER
slave revolt leader

TINA TURNER
entertainer

ALICE WALKER
author

MADAM C. J. WALKER
entrepreneur

BOOKER T. WASHINGTON
educator

DENZEL WASHINGTON
actor

J. C. WATTS
politician

VANESSA WILLIAMS
singer and actress

OPRAH WINFREY
entertainer

TIGER WOODS
golf star

RICHARD WRIGHT
author

ON
ACHIEVEMENT

Coretta Scott King

Before you begin this book, I hope you will ask yourself what the word *excellence* means to you. I think it's a question we should all ask, and keep asking as we grow older and change. Because the truest answer to it should never change. When you think of excellence, perhaps you think of success at work; or of becoming wealthy; or meeting the right person, getting married, and having a good family life.

Those goals are worth striving for, but there is a better way to look at excellence. As Martin Luther King Jr. said in one of his last sermons, "I want you to be first in love. I want you to be first in moral excellence. I want you to be first in generosity. If you want to be important, wonderful. If you want to be great, wonderful. But recognize that he who is greatest among you shall be your servant."

My husband knew that the true meaning of achievement is service. When I met him, in 1952, he was already ordained as a Baptist minister and was working toward a doctoral degree at Boston University. I was studying at the New England Conservatory and dreamed of accomplishments in music. We married a year later, and after I graduated the following year we moved to Montgomery, Alabama. We didn't know it then, but our notions of achievement were about to undergo a dramatic change.

You may have read or heard about what happened next. What began with the boycott of a local bus line grew into a national crusade, and by the time he was assassinated in 1968 my husband had fashioned a black movement powerful enough to shatter forever the practice of racial segregation. What you may not have read about is where he learned to resist injustice without compromising his religious beliefs.

He adopted a strategy of nonviolence from a man of a different race, who lived in a different country and even practiced a different religion. The man was Mahatma Gandhi, the great leader of India, who devoted his life to serving humanity in the spirit of love and nonviolence. It was in these principles that Martin discovered his method for social reform. More than anything else, those two principles were the key to his achievements.

These books are about African Americans who served society through the excellence of their achievements. They form part of the rich history of black men and women in America—a history of stunning accomplishments in every field of human endeavor, from literature and art to science, industry, education, diplomacy, athletics, jurisprudence, even polar exploration.

Not all of the people in this history had the same ideals, but I think you will find that all of them had something in common. Like Martin Luther King Jr., they all decided to become "drum majors" and serve humanity. In that principle—whether it was expressed in books, inventions, or song—they found a goal and a guide outside themselves that showed them a way to serve others instead of living only for themselves.

Reading the stories of these courageous men and women not only helps us discover the principles that we will use to guide our own lives; it also teaches us about our black heritage and about America itself. It is crucial for us to know the heroes and heroines of our history and to realize that the price we paid in our struggle for equality in America was dear. But we must also understand that we have gotten as far as we have partly because America's democratic system and ideals made it possible.

We are still struggling with racism and prejudice. But the great men and women in this series are a tribute to the spirit of the country in which they have flourished. And that makes their stories special and worth knowing.

1

A ROSE IS STILL A ROSE

❦

IN THE WINTER of 1998, the Queen of Soul was invited to sing for opera's greatest tenor, and before the week was out she would do it again, albeit under vastly different circumstances. The setting for the first performance was the Waldorf-Astoria in New York City, where the MusiCares charitable organization held a banquet honoring Italian vocalist Luciano Pavarotti. In attendance was soul singer extraordinaire Aretha Franklin, who had been asked to sing in honor of the legendary Pavarotti. The selection chosen was "Nessun dorma" from the Giacomo Puccini opera *Turandot*. The strikingly haunting aria had long been associated with Pavarotti and was known as one of his signature arias.

After the conclusion of Aretha's passionate performance, the ecstatic Pavarotti rushed to her side and gave her an enthusiastic and grateful embrace. In the course of conversation, he extended to Aretha an invitation to visit his home in Modena, Italy, where, he proposed, they would sing together. Knowing of Franklin's widely publicized fear of flying, the considerate Pavarotti offered to send his private jet for her. He even said he would fly with her from Detroit, where her home is, to Italy, in order to calm any flight anxiety!

Aretha Franklin sings the National Anthem before a 1999 "Three Tenors" concert performance by her friend, Luciano Pavarotti, at Tiger Stadium in Detroit, Michigan.

Aretha Franklin, Luciano Pavarotti, and members of the R&B group Boyz II Men pose for a photograph during a 1998 benefit held in Pavarotti's honor and sponsored by the MusiCares charity in New York City.

Just two days later Aretha Franklin was again performing in New York City, this time at the famed Radio City Music Hall for the Grammy Awards, the music industry's gala annual event. Dressed in a floor-length, red-patterned dress, she rocked the house with a slowed-down reworking of her 1967 classic "Respect," the most popular song of her long career. Aretha had performed the song in the film *Blues Brothers 2000*, the sequel to the 1980 hit film *The Blues Brothers*, in which Franklin had also appeared. This live performance at the Grammy Awards was designed to publicize the new movie, and the four members of the Blues Brothers Band, including Dan Aykroyd and John Goodman, joined her onstage.

After a performance that was received with a standing ovation from her peers, Aretha and the Blues Brothers Band presented the year's Best New Artist Award to singer-songwriter Paula Cole. The grateful Cole, upon receiving her trophy, told the world that receiving this award from the Queen of Soul was like a dream come true. As the program paused for a commercial break, Aretha and the band left the stage, and she headed to her backstage dressing room, where producers of that night's telecast were about to ask Aretha for a favor.

Luciano Pavarotti had been scheduled to sing "Nessun dorma," the same Puccini aria Aretha had performed for him a few days before at the Musi-Cares event. Just minutes before he was to sing, Pavarotti let the producers know that a throat condition had prompted his doctors to warn him against performing. With less than 15 minutes to go before Pavarotti's scheduled performance, the harried producers rushed into Aretha's dressing room and explained the situation. Would she help them out by substituting for the great tenor? After hesitating only a few seconds, Franklin agreed to sing.

"What followed was chaos," Aretha later wrote in her book, *Aretha: From These Roots*. The Grammy staff scrambled to find a tape player on which to play the aria, thus preparing Aretha for the monumental task at hand, which would include reviewing all of the words to the aria. But there were problems. The song had been orchestrated differently from the piece she had sung at the MusiCares benefit. What's more, it was written in Pavarotti's key, much lower than her own. Aretha explained, "There was no time for adjustments or modifications. And certainly no time for rehearsal. This was do or die."

And so she did do it, before an audience of no less than 1.5 billion people watching throughout the world. The response to her triumphant rendering was overwhelmingly positive. "The ovation from my peers was wonderful. I sang Puccini because I love Puccini. It was God who gave me the gift of song, and it is God who keeps me strong in that gift." Aretha Franklin received her second standing ovation of the night.

Aretha has worked with many of today's most successful young stars, including Lauryn Hill, who wrote the title cut for Franklin's album A Rose Is Still a Rose.

But it was not just recording industry insiders who applauded Aretha's surprise performance. People on the streets of New York lavished praise on the singer the following day, as did music critics nationwide. Offers poured in from orchestras all across the United States requesting that Aretha Franklin sing not only her pop hits but also opera with them.

At a press conference held later that week for the release of her album *A Rose Is Still a Rose*, the accolades continued. People were still floored by the stirring performance she had given despite having so little notice. The moment the world would remember best from that awards ceremony belonged to Aretha Franklin. Compliments were also lavished on *Rose*, a successful crossover album on which Aretha had worked with some of the hottest producers of the day, including Lauryn Hill, Sean "Puffy" Combs, and Jermaine Dupri.

"She could probably sing opera if she wanted to," friend and fellow singer Dionne Warwick had predicted about Aretha in the 1988 *American Masters* television documentary "Aretha Franklin: Queen of Soul."

The display of such impressive talent and range of ability shouldn't have come as a surprise to anyone who had been following music or Aretha Franklin's career since the early days. After four decades of illustrious performances—both as a vocalist with an incredible and inimitable voice and as a pianist—the woman referred to as the queen had become both a legend in her own time and true music royalty. From the time 10-year-old Aretha, a shy preacher's daughter, first stood on a chair in her father's church and sang her debut solo, "Jesus, Be a Fence Around Me," the music world—from gospel to soul to pop to opera—would be forever changed.

2

LIFE IN THE CHURCH

JUST AS THE blues, country, and rock and roll music had their storied roots in Memphis, Tennessee, so too did one of the finest interpreters of American music. Aretha Louise Franklin was born in Memphis on March 25, 1942, daughter of Reverend Clarence LaVaughn Franklin and his wife, Barbara Siggers Franklin, a nurse's aide and noted gospel singer. Named for her father's two sisters, Aretha Louise was the fourth child of the couple, whose marriage had already produced two sons, Cecil and Vaughn, and a daughter, Erma. About two years after Aretha's birth, a fifth child, Carolyn Franklin, was born.

A former sharecropper, C. L., as Aretha's father was called, had been drawn to the religious life and then become a Baptist minister at a young age. Years later he would tell his children stories about traveling from point to point in the South of the 1930s, jumping down from the mule he was riding on to preach the Gospel to passersby.

After meeting in Shelby, Mississippi, C. L. and Barbara married and moved to Buffalo, New York, where the young man started what would be a most reputable career as a pastor of the Friendship Baptist Church. He had gone to LeMoyne College in Memphis and studied literature and sociology, an impressive acheivement for an African-American man in the South at that time. From that experience he brought

The daughter of a Baptist minister, Aretha grew up in the church, where she displayed her talents as a gospel singer at a very young age. By the time she was a teenager, she would seek success elsewhere.

forth his more liberal interpretations of the Bible. While at Friendship Baptist Church, Barbara undertook the role of minister's wife and acted as the pianist and choir leader.

When Aretha was two years old, the family moved to Detroit, Michigan, a city which at that time had a bustling economy, due in no small part to the automobile industry. Millions of southerners, especially blacks, had relocated to the city in the hopes of creating a better future. With the move to Detroit came a new assignment for Reverend Franklin—pastorship of the New Bethel Baptist Church.

Life in the Franklin household centered around the church. New Bethel was a large, influential African-American congregation, and the building itself could hold around 4,500 worshippers. As members of the pastor's family, Barbara and the children regularly attended church services, Gospel choir practice, and other church activities. Members of the congregation became like family to the Franklins.

Even visiting gospel singers became well acquainted with the fun-loving Franklin family. Stars of the circuit like Mahalia Jackson (long regarded as the first lady of gospel music), Clara Ward, and Sam Cooke often visited, ate, and worshipped with the Franklins. On one occasion, Aretha was particularly impressed by Nat "King" Cole, a tall, dark, handsome man with a velvety voice singing and playing the family piano. The influences these performers had on the young Aretha would become readily apparent as the years progressed.

Days in the church were filled with Reverend Franklin's powerful and practical sermons and the sweet sound of hymns like "Precious Lord, Take My Hand," "Amazing Grace," and "How I Got Over," one of Clara Ward's trademark songs. Church nurses were on hand in case some parishioners get so caught up in the Spirit that they required smelling salts or some other remedy.

As a child Aretha found inspiration from the many gospel performers who visited her home, including Clara Ward.

The North End of Detroit, in which the Franklins made their home, produced scores of talented young musicians who would soon make their mark in the entertainment industry. Smokey Robinson grew up down the street from the family and was best friends with Cecil Franklin. Diana Ross and the Supremes also lived in the area (although Aretha did not know Diana when they were children). And a young man named Berry Gordy was looking to start a record label in the neighborhood. In 1959 he would found Motown Records, named for the Motor City of Detroit.

As with most families, everything in the Franklin household was not perfect. When Aretha was six years old, her parents separated. The singer talked about this at length for the first time in her autobiography, *Aretha: From These Roots*. "Despite the fact that it has been written innumerable times, it is an absolute lie that my mother abandoned us. In no way, shape, form, or fashion did our mother desert us. She was extremely responsible, loving, and caring. She simply moved with Vaughn back to Buffalo, where she lived with her parents." The Franklins decided that the best plan would be to have the other four children stay with C. L. Barbara Franklin simply would not be able to care for five children on the salary paid to a nurse's aide at Buffalo General Hospital.

Although the separation was hard for the children, it was made easier by regular communication with their mother through phone calls and visits to Buffalo during the summer. Reverend Franklin's mother, Rachel Franklin, whom the family called Big Mama, helped her son out with Cecil, Erma, Aretha, and Carolyn.

Aretha has described herself during these days as a tomboy and a little helper to Big Mama. She loved to climb trees, watch classic 1950s TV like *It's Howdy Doody Time* and *Texaco Star Theatre*, and play pranks on younger sister Carolyn. But something else was increasingly taking up much of young Aretha's time as well: music.

Aretha began piano lessons at the age of eight. In fact, because all of the Franklin children seemed musically oriented, the family owned two pianos. As a result, music was a permanent fixture of the household. Nevertheless, innate talent did not mean that eight-year-old Aretha liked taking lessons. "When my piano teacher came to the house, I would hide behind the coats in the back of the closet because I thought her exercises far too elementary; I wanted to skip to the intermediate level. . . . I wanted to run before I could walk," she admitted later in life. According to Smokey Robinson, Aretha hardly needed lessons at all. In the *American Masters* television special about his friend, he describes the immense piano skills she had as a child as comparable to the ones she exhibits today.

As Ree (as she is sometimes called) became more confident in her piano playing and singing, requests for her to perform increased. Occasionally when Reverend Franklin had guests over who wanted to hear his little girl sing, he would wake Aretha out of a sound sleep, and she would obediently oblige.

In 1952, Aretha's life changed in many important ways. She was baptized at New Bethel Church and sang her first solo there. Standing on a chair to make up for her short stature, the young girl confidently let loose with a rendition of "Jesus, Be a Fence Around Me," a song she had first heard Sam Cooke perform with his gospel group, the Soul Stirrers. The congregation's reaction was a mix of pride and glee. Aretha had heard Clara Ward sing, and after witnessing Ward's passionate vocalizations, the young pastor's daughter knew that one day she would be a singer too.

There was tragedy too, that year, as Barbara Siggers Franklin died suddenly of a heart attack in Buffalo. The children were devastated, especially 10-year-old Aretha. She later wrote: "The pain of small children losing their mother defies description." A very private person by nature, Aretha would rarely speak about the death of her mother in future years.

After the death of Mrs. Franklin, housekeepers and parishioners stepped in to help the family. Big Mama watched over the brood, as did Mahalia Jackson, when she would travel to Detroit, and Reverend Franklin's friend Lola Moore. The family lived in a large six-bedroom-house made of stone, and there was always some activity going on. Aretha has described how Lola and the others would cook delicious meals of soul food for the family, like collard greens, ham hocks, sweet potatoes, and pigs' feet. Thus began Aretha's lifelong love of good cooking.

Within a few years Aretha began to notice young men. One in particular caught her eye, as well as her ear. Aretha was so enamored with Sam Cooke, also the child of a minister, that she sometimes emulated his ways of singing and playing various church songs.

Mahalia Jackson, one of the most influential gospel performers of all time, often helped the Franklin family following the death of Aretha's mother, Barbara.

Reverend Franklin noticed this and chastised his daughter, telling her to sing with her own inner being, instead of copying someone else's style.

In the days before he would become a pop star singing such classics as "You Send Me," "Another Saturday Night," and "We're Having a Party," Sam Cooke and his group, the Soul Stirrers, would appear at New Bethel performing gospel hymns like "Touch the Hem of His Garment" and "Jesus, Be a Fence Around Me." Cooke's smooth voice and delivery and his good looks impressed Aretha greatly, and she developed a crush on the handsome crooner.

Sam Cooke was a powerful presence, but he would not be Aretha Franklin's first love. That honor belonged to a neighborhood boy, a young man Aretha would identify in her autobiography only as "Romeo." (She has never revealed his true name.) At the Arcadia Roller Rink, a favorite hangout, 12-year-old Aretha and Romeo would spend hot summer nights skating for hours listening to the early pop hits of the day.

When she was just 13 Aretha became pregnant with Romeo's child. In the 1950s teen pregnancies were shocking and rare, and rarer still for the daughter of a prominent Baptist pastor. But Reverend Franklin, though a strict father, was supportive when his daughter needed him the most. "Some other fathers have been known to put their daughters out of their homes, but not my dad," Aretha wrote in her memoirs. "He was not judgmental, narrow, or scolding. He simply talked about the responsibilities of motherhood. He was a realist, and he expected me to face the reality of having a child."

Although Romeo and Aretha talked about running away to get married, they never did. During her sixth month of pregnancy, the teenager dropped out of school. Just after turning 14, she gave birth to her son, Clarence, named after her father. To this day the star remains philosophical and spiritual about the early motherhood that faced her in 1956: "All children are gifts from God. All children are miracles. . . . I accepted this blessing . . . The romantic relationship that once burned so brightly burned out. But the love between a mother and a child is forever." Big Mama and Aretha's sister Erma helped the teen care for her infant and watched little Clarence when his mother needed time to herself.

At this time Reverend Franklin's life was undergoing changes of its own. The popular preacher was gaining influence all across the United States, thanks to some sermons that had been aired on Detroit radio stations. The sermons had also been recorded by an independent Chicago recording company called Chess Records, home of some of the famous jazz and blues artists of the 1950s, like Bo Diddley. The reverend became known as "the man with the million-dollar voice," and he began to tour with the popular gospel stars of the era. Religious folks far and wide would come out to school and civic auditoriums to hear Franklin's famous sermons, the most noteworthy among them being "The Eagle Stirreth Her Nest." When C. L. decided to put together his own gospel tour featuring music and sermons, he needed to look no further than his own home for one of his featured performers.

With Clarence in the capable hands of Big Mama, Aretha set out on the tour with her father, in what would be her first professional experience. By singing before the reverend's homilies with the Gospel Caravan, Aretha whetted the appetites of the enthusiastic audiences, many of whom would soon be overcome by the Holy Spirit.

Gospel music is a uniquely American style of song, having grown out of the struggles of Southern slaves in the 19th century. While working in cotton fields or at other labor, slaves would sing phrases back and forth to each other and ask for the Lord's help to survive the tough times ahead. Many blacks hoped for a better future and freedom for themselves and the generations to come. Many gospel songs reflect this belief, referring to a "Promised Land" that could be a United States where slaves were free, Heaven, or both.

Aretha's comfort level as a musician continued to improve, as she was inspired and influenced by another young minister, James Cleveland, who also played piano and sang. In 1956 Chess Records released Aretha's first album, titled *Songs of Faith*, featuring live gospel standards from her performances on the road and at New Bethel. "Three of the songs on that album—'There Is a Fountain Filled with Blood,' 'The Day Is Past and Gone,' and 'While the Blood Runs Warm' are associated with my mentor, Clara Ward. She and Daddy remained my dominant influences," Aretha later recalled. The album wasn't much of a moneymaker, but it earned the Gospel Caravan extra publicity and introduced the reverend's teenage daughter as a church singer of note.

Traveling through the South around 1957 could be dangerous and dehumanizing for blacks, no matter how respected or well-off they were in their own communities. Many public facilities and restaurants did not serve African Americans. "Driving eight or ten hours trying to make a gig, and being hungry and passing restaurants all along the road, and having to go off the road because you're black—that had its effect," Cecil Franklin would later recall. Meeting up with other religious performers like the Staples Singers on the road sometimes made things seem safer for the Franklins.

During the late 1950s and early 1960s the civil rights movement was just beginning. Challenges to the existing social system were often led by a young friend of Reverend Franklin, a minister named Martin Luther King Jr. Reverend Franklin took the young King under his wing and introduced him to many of the influential civic leaders and black people of Detroit.

Blacks all across the country—not just in the largely segregated South—were increasingly demanding equal treatment and equal rights under the law, and the racial tensions that had simmered for years were about to boil over. Reverend King preached about nonviolent protest. Instead of using violence to change the way things were, Martin Luther King and his growing number of supporters used boycotts and "sit-ins" to protest against the system.

Reverend King would often visit with the Franklins both on the road and at their spacious home in Detroit. And every time King saw Aretha he asked her to sing one song in particular for him: "Precious Lord, Take My Hand." It would long be a cherished memory for Aretha.

Around 1956, Aretha's idol Sam Cooke had switched from performing gospel to performing pop music and in 1960 signed a contract with industry giant RCA. Some strict Baptists were disturbed by Cooke's decision, viewing pop and its newly born sibling, rock and roll, as the "devil's music." However, Reverend Franklin was proud of Sam, and so were Aretha and Erma, who had become huge fans of Sam's vocal stylings.

By the time she was 16, Aretha had fallen for another young man she had met at the Arcadia Roller Rink. (The intensely private Aretha has never revealed his name.) In time she was pregnant with her second child, Edward. Again, the reverend and the entire Franklin family supported Ree.

As Reverend Franklin's fame increased, the Gospel Caravan made trips to more urban parts of the country, including Los Angeles, where they visited Sam Cooke at his new home.

Aretha was so impressed by Sam Cooke's success that she began giving deeper thought to her own future musical prospects. She explained, "Before my eighteenth birthday, the path ahead seemed clear: I would test the waters and venture forth into the world of popular music. If Sam could make it, perhaps I could too."

When Aretha saw gospel singer Sam Cooke make a successful transition to pop music, she decided to explore "the world of popular music" as well.

3

THE COLUMBIA YEARS

❧

IN 1960 ARETHA Franklin and her father set out on their quest for secular, or nonreligious, stardom for the 18-year-old. The preacher encouraged his daughter's growing interest in a pop music career, despite the protests of some within the church community who felt that Aretha was abandoning her gospel roots.

When fellow Detroit resident Berry Gordy expressed interest in signing Ree to his newly born label, Motown, both of the Franklins thought that a larger, more experienced label was the route to go. They headed to New York City, where Aretha eventually rented an apartment.

One of the first things Aretha and C. L. Franklin did was cut a demonstration record to circulate among the record companies. With the assistance of a Detroit bass player named Major Holley, and three professional studio musicians who provided backup, Aretha performed old standards, including "My Funny Valentine," and newer compositions, like "Today I Sing the Blues."

Aretha acquired an agent by the name of Jo King, who was instrumental in getting the demo into the hands of John Hammond, a producer at Columbia Records, one of the largest national and international music labels at that time. Legend had it that Hammond, a member of the wealthy Vanderbilt family, had discovered jazz greats Billie Holiday and Count Basie during his tenure at the company.

During the 1960s, Aretha stepped out from her home in Detroit and headed east to New York City, home to many of the recording industry's biggest labels.

Jazz legend Billie Holiday performs "Fine and Mellow" onstage. Columbia Records producer John Hammond referred to Aretha as "untutored genius, the best natural singer since Billie Holiday."

John Hammond described his reaction upon hearing the demo: "One day a black composer arrived at my office with a demonstration record of various songs he had written. The fourth one particularly caught my ear. . . . It was called 'Today I Sing the Blues,' and performed by a young woman who accompanied herself on piano. . . . Her name was Aretha Franklin, and even at first hearing, on a poorly made demo intended to sell songs rather than the singer, she was the most dynamic jazz voice I'd encountered since Billie [Holiday]."

Almost immediately Hammond offered Aretha Franklin a recording contract with Columbia Records. Unbeknownst to Aretha, Sam Cooke was also trying to recruit her for the record label he was signed to, RCA. "While Daddy and I were talking to Columbia . . . I never knew of Sam's interest," she wrote in 1999. "I have a feeling that if Sam had caught up with me, I would have gone to RCA. But it wasn't meant to be." Aretha signed the contract with Columbia.

John Hammond took care of all the arrangements for and produced the first album, which would eventually be called *Aretha*. Working with some of the top New York session musicians of the early 1960s, Aretha recorded the Judy Garland gem "Over the Rainbow," "Today I Sing the Blues," "Maybe I'm a Fool," "Right Now," and other selections. "Aretha sang and played her heart out. . . . the resulting masterpiece crossed the bridges between blues, jazz, pop, and gospel," wrote journalist David Nathan in *The Soulful Divas*. But the album was not a financial success.

Aretha continued to work on her poise, vocals, and choreography. As Big Mama and Erma looked after Clarence and Eddie back in Detroit, Aretha focused on her musical aspirations.

While old friend Smokey Robinson and his Miracles were churning out hits for themselves and other Motown acts, Aretha steadily worked and recorded. But the hits were not coming, and she made little money. Aretha remained optimistic, as she recalled, "Personally, I was simply thrilled to have a contract with a major company. I was also thrilled with the high level of musicianship surrounding me. Hammond—and, for that matter, everyone I worked with at Columbia—recruited the best studio players and background singers around."

For a while, Aretha chose not to be concerned about her hitless status. Instead she concentrated on her live shows. She performed night after night, but not at the famous Apollo Theater in Harlem—only stars with hits performed there. Aretha made the rounds of clubs in New York and other cities, including Philadelphia and Chicago.

Although Aretha was certainly not a household name in the early 1960s, people—including music critics—were starting to take notice of the young black woman with the bluesy, smokey, passionate voice. She was starting to sing in a style that would become her hallmark, she noted: "Looking back, I see that I was . . . developing a vocal signature. It wasn't something I did consciously. And it wasn't part of a plan. It was simply me."

While playing a succession of jazz clubs, Aretha sometimes got the opportunity to tour with her favorite male singer, Sam Cooke. Another time she made the rounds of the rhythm and blues clubs (referred to as the "chitlin' circuit") with Jackie Wilson, a popular vocalist at the time and a friend of Vaughn and Cecil Franklin. Each tour required performers to play 28 gigs in a row. Although the exposure and the experiences were valuable, Aretha found that she did not enjoy performing in a different city every night. She decided to keep her tours to more manageable lengths of time in the future.

Meanwhile, misdirection at Columbia Records continued to plague Aretha's career. Her single releases were "turntable hits" or "jukebox hits"—they received a lot of radio airplay but they did not sell well. Other artists had singles that did both. Executives at the label had her singing everything from Broadway show tunes to jazz to pop standards. Aretha certainly was not easy to pigeonhole into one genre in those days. Even she sometimes chose songs that might not have been the perfect match for what she was trying to accomplish at this time—making a name for herself in one of the most challenging industries in the world. While contemporaries were performing new-sounding, sometimes groundbreaking material, she was singing lots of "covers"— songs already recorded by other artists.

In 1961, while Aretha was visiting family in Detroit, her sister Erma introduced her to a man named Ted White. The two started dating, frequently going to the hottest nightclubs in the Motor City, and soon things became serious. "Ted White knew his way around Detroit. He was a take-charge kind of guy, and before I knew it he had become my manager," she later wrote.

Although Aretha knew that her new boyfriend continued to date other women, she still trusted him. After a short time they were married in Ohio by a justice of the peace. According to some accounts, Reverend Franklin did not approve of the union and was often at odds with the controlling Ted White. After a few years of marriage, the couple had a son, Ted White Jr.

When John Hammond's role as producer came to an end, Aretha began working with arranger Bob Mersey, who continued to steer the singer toward traditional pop favorites. With Mersey,

Aretha recorded covers of "Try a Little Tenderness," the sweet Jimmy Durante tune "Make Someone Happy," and "If Ever I Would Leave You" from Camelot, one of the most popular Broadway musicals of the early 1960s. Her second album was known as *The Electrifying Aretha Franklin*, but it did little to spark sales.

In 1963 singer Dinah Washington died of an accidental overdose of alcohol and drugs. Soon after, Aretha was approached by Columbia and asked to record a tribute to the late "Queen of the Blues." She quickly agreed and made the album *Unforgettable: A Tribute to Dinah Washington*, released the following year. *Unforgettable* was a minor success, but now is a prized collector's item for Aretha devotees.

The British Invasion first struck around 1963 and 1964, with young rock and rollers like the Beatles and the Rolling Stones (who both claimed African-American influences) conquering America. But there was another musical movement also taking place in the United States. With artists such as the Supremes, the Four Tops, and Mary Wells, Motown founder Berry Gordy was spearheading a revolution of his own.

In the years Aretha had been recording for Columbia, Gordy's Detroit company, Motown Records, had begun filling a gap in the music world and making history at the same time. As black people strove to obtain more freedom and opportunities throughout the country, they also cried out for more representation in popular culture. Motown heard the call and

The success of Motown acts like the Supremes led Columbia Records to promote Aretha Franklin's work more aggressively.

An appearance on The Ed Sullivan Show, *such as this one by the Beatles, often turned artists into stars overnight. It was very disappointing to Aretha when her scheduled appearance on the show was called off.*

answered back with popular hits like "My Girl," "You Better Shop Around," and "Please Mr. Postman." As Gordy's business slowly became an empire, the time seemed right for Aretha's career at Columbia to mirror those of her Motown counterparts.

Columbia executives decided to promote Aretha Franklin more aggressively and commercially after the release of the *Unforgettable* album. To that end, they hired Clyde Otis to produce Aretha's next album. Otis, who had also worked with Dinah Washington, oversaw the production of another popular turntable single, "Runnin' Out of Fools," which became a Top 60 single and the name of the album. Aretha also recorded a version of Mary Wells's "My Guy," written by family friend Smokey Robinson, but her version of the song went nowhere.

While Clyde Otis and Ted White tussled, Aretha was booked on *The Ed Sullivan Show* for the first time. She couldn't have been more thrilled, and there couldn't have been a better remedy for her stalled career. After appearing on *Ed Sullivan*, the most popular variety show in the country for many years, new artists like Elvis Presley, the Beatles, and others had become famous literally overnight.

Aretha was scheduled to sing the romantic ballad "Skylark" and an up-tempo version of the hit song from *Breakfast at Tiffany's*, "Moon River." However, there was a problem: someone at the show thought that Aretha's dress, a silk number with orange-gold beads specially made by a Detroit designer, was too revealing. Although Aretha did not agree, she nonetheless changed into another gown that she had brought along. Then Aretha waited to be called onstage. Minutes went by, and finally she was approached again by another show staffer who broke the news: she would not be performing that night after all. The show had been overbooked. The disappointed Aretha left the studio in tears.

One good thing came out of the *Ed Sullivan* experience. Aretha soon began to get bookings for other popular TV programs like *Shindig* and *American Bandstand*, two popular music showcases that appealed to 1960s teenagers. Appearances on these shows could only help her career.

Meanwhile, back in Detroit, many changes were taking place. The New Bethel Baptist Church building had been torn down to make room for a highway and the congregation had to relocate several times. Finally, the church was reestablished in an old theater building at the corners of Linwood and Philadelphia Boulevards in the city. Rev. C. L. Franklin's involvement with the civil rights movement and with Rev. Martin Luther King Jr. increased. In 1963 Franklin helped organize a march in Detroit with King that became the model for a larger march held in Washington, D.C., later that same year. King delivered his historic and moving "I Have a Dream" speech in Detroit before delivering it in Washington. Aretha became more involved in the civil rights struggle as well, performing at fund-raisers.

Aretha's road to stardom received some early help from appearances on television shows such as American Bandstand, *hosted by Dick Clark.*

As Aretha's star began to climb, she played the Newport Jazz Festival and the New York Jazz Festival, sharing the stage with up-and-coming stars like Ike and Tina Turner and veteran performers like Dizzy Gillespie. At the same time her father kept her feet firmly on the ground. "I would come home to visit, and I didn't feel like I should have to share the housework . . . everyone would be working, washing dishes and vacuuming . . . and I would be standing around. . . . my dad came downstairs . . . and he said, 'See if you can find your way in that kitchen and introduce yourself to the trash,'" Aretha later recalled.

In December 1964 Aretha's father called her with some sad news: Sam Cooke had been shot and killed. Aretha was devastated by the death of yet another musical mentor, one who had been a true friend and on whom she had one of her first childhood crushes. "Aretha went berserk," recalled musician Teddy

Harris, who had been playing a show with her in Atlanta the night Sam was killed. "After all the customers and employees had gone home from the club, she made all the musicians in her group stay . . . and she played Sam Cooke's music on the piano for four hours."

Although Aretha remained relatively hitless, Columbia extended her contract, and she continued to record albums, with titles like *Aretha Sings the Blues* and *Sweet Bitter Love*. She still garnered praise from critics, and disc jockeys played her singles, but people were not buying them. By the mid-1960s, Aretha had become increasingly unhappy with the situation. "They know and they know that I know that they haven't given me the same 'big buildup' that they've given say Robert Goulet or Barbra Streisand," Aretha told *Ebony* in 1964.

It seemed like the time was right for a change.

The sudden death of friend and mentor Sam Cooke shocked 22-year-old Aretha. Cooke's funeral service drew many prominent members of the musical community.

THE 1968 DEMOCRATIC NATIONAL CONVENTION CHICAGO ILLINOIS

4

R-E-S-P-E-C-T

Aretha opens the second session of the 1968 Democratic National Convention by singing the National Anthem.

Word SPREAD QUICKLY that Aretha Franklin's contract at Columbia was coming up for renewal and that she was not interested in staying with the label. In early 1966 Louise Bishop, a well-known Philadelphia disc jockey and an acquaintance of Aretha's, called her friend Jerry Wexler in Alabama to report the news.

At the time, Wexler, a producer at Atlantic Records, was recording with artist Wilson Pickett in the legendary blues town of Muscle Shoals. After hanging up the phone, Wexler, a longtime Aretha fan from her *Songs of Faith* days, immediately set the wheels in motion to sign her.

"I called Aretha that minute and set up a meeting in New York," Wexler wrote almost 30 years later. At a meeting with Aretha and husband/manager Ted White, Jerry Wexler offered Aretha a $30,000 signing bonus. Although she felt a bit cautious at first, she signed with Atlantic soon afterward. "With all the fine records I had made at Columbia, I wasn't sure how I would like Atlantic, but I was willing to try. I wanted a hit, and I wanted to be with a company that understood the current market. . . . Right from the start, I felt good about the arrangement."

For one thing, Atlantic was relatively familiar to Aretha. Many of her favorite R&B performers from childhood, including Ray Charles, Ruth Brown, and the Drifters, were Atlantic Records acts. Also, by 1966, the first musicians to play soul music were getting noticed—Wilson Pickett, the Young Rascals, and Otis Redding, among others. It was a place where Aretha felt she could make the records that would be true hits—those that would sell.

Because Jerry Wexler was busy producing other artists at the time, he offered Jim Stewart, an executive at Atlantic subsidiary Stax Records, the chance to produce Aretha's recordings. Stewart declined, leaving Wexler in charge and keeping Aretha an Atlantic act, while her soul music contemporaries like Sam & Dave and Otis Redding recorded on the Stax label.

With the personal attention provided by Jerry Wexler, Aretha set about finding and writing songs to record for her Atlantic debut album. Meanwhile Wexler made arrangements for her to record at Fame Studios in Muscle Shoals, the same facility he used for Wilson Pickett.

Wexler has been widely quoted as saying that in that part of the South he had found a "wonderful rhythm section of white Alabama country boys who took a left turn to the blues," the perfect backing section for his newly signed artist. While another musician played organ, Aretha played acoustic piano, something she hadn't done much of in her Columbia days. Indeed, Aretha later wrote that "putting me back on piano helped Aretha-ize the new music."

Jerry Wexler agreed. "I would never have dreamed of developing tracks without Aretha rooted at the piano; that's what made her material organic. She'd find the key, devise the rhythm pattern, then work out the background vocals, a critical ingredient, with her sisters Carolyn and Erma and/or the Sweet Inspirations." The Sweet Inspirations were a gospel group led by Cissy Houston, mother of future star Whitney Houston, who also recorded with the likes of Elvis Presley.

On January 24, 1967, recording on the album began at Fame Studios. The first song to be recorded was "I Never Loved a Man (The Way I Love You)," an Aretha-penned tune and eventually the title of the first Atlantic album. While many of the melodies, harmonies, and orchestrations had been worked out before the actual recording, there was still a sense of spontaneity present in the studio as well. Aretha rejoiced in the creative atmosphere, and it clearly worked for her.

According to Jerry Wexler, "the minute Aretha touched the piano and sang a note, the musicians were awestruck. They raced for their instruments and caught her fever. 'I've never experienced so much feeling coming from one human being,' said [drummer] Roger Hawkins. 'When she hit that first chord, we knew everything was going to be all right,'" commented another witness to Aretha's soul-stirring performance.

But everything was not all right. A disagreement between Ted White and a session player had turned into a heated argument and finally a physical altercation back at the musicians' hotel. Aretha and her husband ended up leaving Alabama the next day, with neither of them speaking a word about the circumstances on the flight back to New York.

Aretha's producer was in shock and in a panic. He possessed just one completed song from the historic session, "I Never Loved a Man," and pieces of a second song, "Do Right Woman—Do Right Man," which contained no piano playing or vocals from Aretha. Back in New York with only half of a single record release available, Wexler distributed a few copies to some influential disc jockeys. They loved the finished song. All Wexler had to do was find Aretha and fast.

This was no small challenge. Upon returning to New York City, the Whites had broken up, and Wexler could not get in contact with either of them. Within a few weeks, Aretha, back together with Ted, resurfaced and finished the recording of "Do Right Woman" in New York with the same studio musicians from Muscle Shoals, except for the one who had fought with Ted White. Things went very smoothly, and Wexler involved engineer Tom Dowd and arranger Arif Marden, two men who would become increasingly important in Aretha's recording career.

The single of "I Never Loved a Man" with the flip side of "Do Right Woman" became Aretha's first million-selling record. It rose to number nine on the pop charts and number thirty-seven on the R&B charts. Aretha Franklin at last had a real hit.

But while that record was being played constantly on the radio and by fans on their turntables at home, Aretha was still busy working on *I Never Loved a Man*. The album would contain perhaps the most important song of her career and the one that would be forever identified with her.

Taking an Otis Redding ditty that had charted for him back in 1965 and infusing it with classic rhythms, sexy phrasing, and just plain soul, Aretha recorded "Respect" on Valentine's Day 1967. She and Carolyn Franklin had come up with the line "Sock it to me," sung in rapid repetition toward the middle of the song. The line "Sock it to me" became even more famous when it was regularly used on the TV comedy series *Laugh-In*.

Aretha's recording of "Respect" took on another aspect of social significance, too, as the country came to grips with the issues of civil rights for blacks and equal rights for women. The song became a rallying cry for both groups.

Today, "Respect" is still Aretha's most requested song in concert and the one that gets the greatest response. Released on April 16, 1967, the anthem shot to number one on both the pop and R&B charts. For two weeks "Respect" was the number one pop song in America. All told, the song spent an impressive 11 weeks in the Top 40. With the

release of "Respect," Aretha Franklin became a household name. Other hits on the album included "Save Me," cowritten by Carolyn Franklin, and the Aretha and Ted White composition "Dr. Feelgood (Love Is a Serious Business)."

The recording industry took notice, too. Aretha was honored by the National Academy of Recording Arts and Sciences with two Grammy Awards for "Respect"—one for Best Rhythm and Blues Recording and one for Best Rhythm and Blues Solo Vocal Performance, Female. Critics and magazines declared Aretha a star, and she won numerous accolades as the "Female Singer of the Year" for 1967.

Aretha didn't rest on her laurels, though. Before the year was out, Atlantic had released a second album, *Aretha Arrives*, which showed a pensive Aretha on the cover and featured versions of earlier songs like the Rolling Stones' "(I Can't Get No) Satisfaction" and the R&B hit "Baby I Love You." Carolyn and Erma provided backing vocals, as did Aretha's cousin Brenda Corbett and the Sweet Inspirations.

In addition to recording sessions, live performances kept Aretha busy. Aretha is seen here with fellow musicians King Curtis (left) and Joe Tex after a concert in 1968.

Aretha performed the hymn "Precious Lord, Take My Hand" at the funeral for the Reverend Martin Luther King Jr. following his assassination in 1968.

Soul (which was also an honorary title for Aretha), was released in January and contained two smash hits, "Chain of Fools" (the number two pop song for two weeks in a row) and "(You Make Me Feel Like) A Natural Woman," a song whose writers included Jerry Wexler and Carole King. Aretha continued working with the Muscle Shoals musicians and was also joined by Duane Allman, later a member of the Allman Brothers Band, and Eric Clapton, then a member of the group Cream.

Less than six months later, another Aretha Franklin album was unleashed on a willing public. Titled *Aretha Now*, the album was another huge success. With her recording "I Say a Little Prayer for You," previously a hit for Dionne Warwick, Aretha scored again. The song was a Top 10 hit and her seventh gold single. It also spent ten weeks in the Top 40. "Think," a cautionary anthem about love written by Ted White and his wife with a repeated chorus of "Freedom, freedom, freedom . . . freedom," became a number one R&B hit and did well on the pop charts too. And in tribute to the late great Sam Cooke, Aretha recorded an impassioned version of his hit "You Send Me." Both *Lady Soul* and *Aretha Now* were gold albums, selling in excess of 500,000 copies each.

A third 1968 album, *Aretha in Paris*, was recorded on a tour that also included stops in Germany, Holland, and England. Released in October of that year, the recording gave an additional boost to Aretha's career. *Cash Box*, *Billboard*, and *Record World* magazines honored her with awards after the album's release.

Earlier in the year Aretha had been featured in a *Time* magazine cover story that discussed the soul music phenomenon. Aretha was not pleased with the magazine's portrayal of her as a slave to the blues, like her forerunners, Bessie Smith and Billie Holiday. *Time* also got the story wrong when it claimed that Aretha's mother had "abandoned" the family. For years afterward, Aretha had a distrust for journalists that has only recently abated.

The *Time* article did get one thing correct, however, when it hinted that there was trouble in Aretha's marriage. By the end of the 1960s, Aretha and Ted White were divorced, and he was replaced as her manager. White profited handsomely from the marriage, receiving half of the copyrights from the songs that Aretha had recorded. Aretha was said to be badly depressed over the final breakup with Ted, and she missed some scheduled shows, prompting rumors about her emotional and physical health.

With the monumental successes of 1967 and 1968 behind her, Aretha Franklin had surely arrived as one of the premier performers of soul music. The question on everyone's mind was, where would she go from here?

5

AMAZING GRACE

ONE DAY, a short time after her marriage to Ted White ended, the Motown group the Temptations showed up unannounced at Aretha's front door in Detroit. The members wanted to record some songs with her. One of the better known Temptations, Dennis Edwards, and Aretha were immediately attracted to each other. Despite her brother Cecil's warnings that Edwards was a bit too much of a ladies' man, Aretha encouraged the relationship. As it eventually turned out, the relationship with Edwards was short-lived, but it helped her get used to life again as a single woman.

In the late 1960s Aretha was invited by a group of young, upwardly mobile black businessmen to join them in their investment firm. Calling themselves the New Breeders, the entrepreneurs designed and manufactured a line of clothing and accessories in the African tradition. One member of the group was a slim man named Ken Cunningham, who was separated from his wife and the father of a young girl. He had a tall Afro and wore a *dashiki*, a traditional African garment.

Years later Aretha would recall their initial meeting as love at first sight. She would even sometimes refer to Ken as her alter-ego, because of the ways their personalities meshed. According to Aretha,

Aretha won her eighth Grammy Award for her work on the gospel recording Amazing Grace.

meeting "Wolf" (as she nicknamed him) had many positive effects: "I blossomed under his strong support. . . Wolf even helped me change my approach to makeup. I stopped shaving my eyebrows and using pencils and went back to a natural look with a much lighter touch. I lost weight and wore my hair in an Afro; I began to appreciate myself as a beautiful black woman."

Back in the studio, Aretha recorded *Soul '69*, an album largely made up of jazzy versions of some old favorite compositions. She recorded "Today I Sing the Blues" a second time (the first was for her Columbia debut), "Tracks of My Tears" by Smokey Robinson, and "Crazy He Calls Me."

In 1969 Aretha was elated to be asked to sing at the Academy Awards. She brought along Ken, her wardrobe mistress, and her father for the occasion. After being introduced by Frank Sinatra, Aretha let loose with a masterful rendition of the song "Funny Girl," which had been nominated for an Oscar.

In January 1970 Atlantic released Aretha's seventh album for the company, *This Girl's in Love with You*, which featured the title song, "Son of a Preacher Man," and two Beatles songs, "Let It Be" and "Eleanor Rigby." While anyone would be hard-pressed to top the Beatles' original versions of these songs, Aretha gave the group a run for its money with her gospel- and blues-tinged versions. She explained how greatly she respected John Lennon and Paul McCartney as songwriters: "The minute I heard ["Let It Be"] . . . I loved it. Ditto for "Eleanor Rigby." Early on I recognized the Beatles' charm as showmen and their talent as writers."

This Girl's in Love with You went gold, and the song "Share Your Love with Me" went to the top position on the R&B charts. "Eleanor Rigby" went to number five R&B, and "The Weight" a song originated by the Band, was a number three R&B single.

In 1970, Aretha and Ken's son was born. They named him Kecalf (pronounced "Kelf"), which is an amalgam of the initials of their names: Ken E. Cunningham and Aretha L. Franklin. Aretha and Ken moved with Kecalf into a large brownstone that they had purchased in New York City, while Aretha's two oldest boys, Clarence and Eddie, stayed with Big Mama in Detroit. Ted Jr. lived with his father and his father's mother. Not long after, the boys came to live with Aretha, Ken, and Kecalf in New York, where they were enrolled in a private school.

Ken became Aretha's road manager, and Cecil Franklin, by this time an assistant pastor at New Bethel, joined his sister's management team.

Aretha kept busy recording her second album of the new decade, *Spirit in the Dark*, for which she wrote the title song. Upon the release of the album, a music critic from the *New York Times* wrote that he wondered if Aretha was even capable of making a bad album. "Don't Play That Song," cowritten by Atlantic Records founder Ahmet Ertegun, whom Aretha greatly admired, was featured on the album and went to number one on the R&B charts and number eleven on the pop list.

In late July 1970 Aretha made another tour of the United Kingdom and was well received by her audiences. While in England, Aretha also appeared on the TV show *Top of the Pops*, a showcase for the latest acts and their hit songs, and sang "Don't Play That Song."

Aretha poses for a photo with her son, Kecalf, who was born in 1970.

"Wolf called [this period] the Age of Aretha," Aretha wrote. "I loved that phrase, by which he meant people were growing up to my music, getting married, having babies, defining their youth and making memories that would last a lifetime. I loved being part of all those memories."

The following fall Aretha started recording tracks for her next studio album, *Young, Gifted and Black*. But before that album was completed, Jerry Wexler, booked Aretha at the Fillmore West Theater in San Francisco. In 1971 the city had a reputation as a home to hippies and "flower children," and both Aretha and Wexler were unsure of how a San Francisco audience would react to this soul-singing black woman. Aretha's music was definitely different from what they were used to hearing.

It turned out that Aretha and Jerry's concerns were groundless. On February 7, 1971, the Fillmore West was packed with an open-minded, peace-loving audience, at least double the number the 5,000-seat theater could hold. Aretha carefully selected songs she thought the crowd of young people would enjoy, from the Stephen Stills' smash "Love the One You're With" to the Beatles' "Eleanor Rigby" to Simon and Garfunkel's masterpiece, "Bridge Over Troubled Water." Of course, the obligatory Aretha hits were part of the show too. The crowd cheered and swayed to "Respect," "Dr. Feelgood," and "Don't Play That Song." Bouquets of flowers were thrown onstage to the singer.

When Aretha found out that her good friend, singer and songwriter Ray Charles, was in the audience, she went into the crowd and brought him on stage where they sang a duet of her composition "Spirit in the Dark." The audience roared and clapped its approval, although Charles obviously didn't know all the lyrics.

According to the astrology-minded Aretha, "All the planets were aligned right that night, because when the music came down, it was as real and righteous as any recording I'd ever made." Several times

Aretha has noted that her performance at the Fillmore was one of her career highlights.

In May 1971 Atlantic released *Live at Fillmore West*, which soon became another gold album, and Aretha was awarded a Grammy Award for Best R&B Vocal Performance, Female, for her cover of "Bridge Over Troubled Water." It was her sixth Grammy trophy in just five years and her fourth in this category. (For years, Aretha had asked Jerry Wexler to go to the annual ceremony and accept the awards on her behalf. It wasn't until a few years after her breakthrough that Aretha began regularly attending the Grammys.)

Aretha's exhilarating performances helped to add to the growing excitement generated by her music. She performs here on a 1971 episode of the television show Soul Train.

In January 1972 Aretha released *Young, Gifted and Black,* an album that was a resounding critical, commercial, and artistic success. The work symbolized how black Americans were feeling at the beginning of the 1970s: Their struggle was not over, but clearly some gains had been made. The death of Martin Luther King Jr. had left its scars, but with the new decade came new hopes and new dreams. It was the era of black pride, the era about which Reverend Franklin had long preached in his sermons.

Today Aretha calls the album one of her most personal and perhaps most romantic. Critics and music fans called it one of the most original and creative recorded works they had heard in a long time. Apparently Ken Cunningham's advice to Aretha to be herself and to act naturally was working. She felt more open to creative risks.

Young, Gifted and Black contained "First Snow in Kokomo," one of Aretha's poems set to music; another

Beatles cover, "The Long and Winding Road"; the title tune (written and first recorded by performer Nina Simone, whom many compared to Aretha in the 1960s); and Aretha's own "Rock Steady."

The same month that *Young, Gifted and Black* was released, Aretha lost another one of her mentors, and the world of gospel music lost its pearl when Mahalia Jackson died on January 27, 1972. Aretha and her father attended the funeral at Chicago's McCormick Place, along with 6,000 other mourners. Although Jackson and Reverend Franklin had apparently had their differences and grown apart over the years, the Franklins felt it was their duty to pay their respects to the woman who had sometimes been a surrogate mother to the Franklin children. Aretha did one other thing: she sang for Mahalia, just as she had sung for Martin Luther King, "Precious Lord, Take My Hand."

In an unusual way, Aretha's hymn honoring Mahalia Jackson coincided with what was to be her next project. For years Jerry Wexler had been trying to get Aretha to record a gospel album. Aretha had repeatedly declined, but in early 1972 the time finally seemed right. Aretha reflected on how it felt to make her recording in church: "It's a feeling you get there you just don't get anywhere else."

Aretha has always steadfastly denied that she ever "left" the gospel community or her religion in general. "[The album] *Amazing Grace* took me back to church and to the King of Gospel, the Reverend James Cleveland," Aretha recollected in her autobiography. "When I say 'took me back to church,' I mean recording in church. I never left church. And never will. Church is as much a part of me as the air I breathe. I have heard people say that one singer or another 'gave up gospel for pop.' That is not my case. . . . I expanded, but I never abandoned [the church]."

Over two incredible nights in January 1972 at Los Angeles's New Temple Missionary Baptist Church, Aretha, Rev. James Cleveland, and the

Southern California Community Choir committed *Amazing Grace* to tape. If any of the people present once thought Aretha had left the church behind, they certainly welcomed her back with open arms that night.

Rev. C. L. Franklin told the congregation that he was "about to bust wide open" with the anticipation of hearing his daughter sing gospel music again. Arif Mardin, who had worked on many Atlantic albums with Aretha, said, "It was so incredible. Aretha got extremely emotional doing some of the songs and she had to sit . . . and kind of reflect."

The finished album would contain a plethora of gospel classics, like "Mary, Don't You Weep," "Precious Lord, Take My Hand," Clara Ward's signature hymn "How I Got Over," and a 10-minute version of "Amazing Grace." But Aretha also included such secular songs as Carole King's "You've Got a Friend" and Richard Rodgers and Oscar Hammerstein's "You'll Never Walk Alone."

The Reverend James Cleveland worked with Aretha on the 1972 album Amazing Grace, *which saw her return to her gospel roots.*

The album was an overwhelming success upon release and would eventually become the best-selling gospel album of all time, with more than two million copies sold. The double-album was also Aretha's biggest seller.

The National Academy of Recording Arts and Sciences awarded Aretha her eighth Grammy Award for *Amazing Grace*. She also won her ninth Grammy that year, for *Young, Gifted and Black*, but Aretha gave the award to fellow singer Esther Phillips, who had also been nominated and was having personal problems at the time.

Aretha has stood by her belief that all people—black or white—should be treated equally. Once, at a photo shoot for *Vogue* magazine, Aretha was unhappy to find that all of the models she was to be photographed with were white. Aretha walked out, with Ken Cunningham in tow. It was the first time she had ever walked out on a photo shoot.

Before she embarked on a tour of the U.S. Virgin Islands and Africa in the early 1970s Aretha told an interviewer that her tour contract had an unusual stipulation: the audiences must either be fully integrated or black only. She refused to play for a segregated, all-white audience.

Back in the United States, Aretha recorded her twelfth Atlantic album, *Hey Now Hey (The Other Side of the Sky)*, which was released in the summer of 1973. The recording was produced by musician Quincy Jones, but it did not reflect the Aretha that the public had grown to know and appreciate. Less commercial than her previous albums, it was not received well, but the single "Angel," written by Carolyn Franklin, became Aretha's 13th number one R&B single.

That same year Aretha lost yet another friend and inspiration. Clara Ward, Aretha's most influential female mentor, died at age 48. As was her custom, Aretha performed at the funeral, this time singing a song that Clara had once sung, "The Day Is Past and Gone."

During the 1970s, when not in the recording studio, Aretha performed live in nightclubs, mostly in California and New York. She worked a variety of elements into her shows, experimenting with costumes and choreography, and giving vocal impressions of fellow artists Diana Ross and Gladys Knight. While taking courses in ballet, Aretha found ways to work those new skills into the concerts too. The response was usually good.

Whether or not her audiences liked her ever-changing flamboyant stage costumes was a different story. Aretha took some ribbing for the outfits she picked to wear in her live shows, but she claimed not to be bothered by the criticism. While political statements were of no interest to her, fashion statements were. And she was certainly saying something by wearing *dashikis* to photo sessions, sequined lavender jumpsuits in concert, or a clown outfit complete with red nose while performing "That's Entertainment" at Radio City Music Hall in 1974.

A song Stevie Wonder wrote for Aretha, "Until You Come Back to Me (That's What I'm Gonna Do)" was a number three pop hit and was featured on her 1974 release *Let Me in Your Life*. It was the first album on which Aretha received a coproducer credit.

Having won another Grammy in 1973 for the song "Master of Eyes," Aretha was rewarded again the following year. She took home the coveted award for her recording of the Nickolas Ashford and Valerie Simpson classic "Ain't Nothing Like the Real Thing," which appeared on *Let Me in Your Life*.

In total, from 1967 to 1974, Aretha won a Grammy for Best R&B Vocal Performance, Female, eight times—every time she was nominated. However, Aretha's future albums would be less commercial. And as Atlantic Records started to show more interest in rock music, it looked less and less likely that Aretha could continue her winning streak, with her albums or her Grammy wins.

6

CHANGES

⟨♦⟩

WITH A SLUMP in her record sales becoming apparent in 1974, Aretha and Atlantic tried some new approaches to her music. Most were unsuccessful. According to David Nathan, author of *The Soulful Divas* and the journalist who has interviewed Aretha more than any other, "For better or worse, Aretha [became] much more involved with producing her own albums, and she tended toward a certain vocal self-indulgence."

The follow-up to *Let Me in Your Life*, *With Everything I Feel in Me*, did nothing to pull Aretha out of the downturn her career seemed to be in. The collection of songs failed to make the Top 40—it was the first time that had happened since Aretha signed with Atlantic. Jerry Wexler's involvement had steadily declined, and Aretha looked to other writers and producers for fresh material.

Two young songwriters, Chuck Jackson (brother of Franklin family friend Rev. Jesse Jackson) and Marvin Yancy, were interested in recording with Lady Soul and offered her an array of songs to record. Although Aretha liked what she heard, she didn't feel that the material was right for her. As a result, Jackson and Yancy brought some of the songs to an up-and-coming singer named Natalie Cole.

The daughter of famed musician Nat "King" Cole, Natalie was a relative newcomer to the music industry. She was looking for material to record on

In addition to her live shows Aretha appeared on TV specials throughout the 1970s. She is seen here singing on a Bob Hope special in 1975.

her debut album for Capitol Records. Two of the songs first presented to Aretha, "This Will Be," and "I've Got Love on My Mind," were later recorded by Natalie Cole, and became hits. In interviews she gave in the mid-1970s, Natalie Cole mentioned Aretha as an influence, although she maintained that Chaka Kahn, lead singer of the band Rufus, was her real inspiration.

With Aretha in the first dry spell in her career, and with Natalie Cole being hailed by some in the press as the successor to the Queen of Soul, the situation looked ripe for a quarrel according to some industry observers. When Aretha failed to win the Best R&B Vocal Performance Grammy in 1976, the rumors of a bitter feud between the two women became so common that Natalie addressed them in public. Aretha offered no comment at the time, but in her 1999 memoir felt the need to set the record straight. "They say imitation is the sincerest form of flattery. In fact, when the Women of the Five Boroughs of New York honored me, [Natalie] sang for me. I sent her flowers and welcomed her into the industry. But some industry magazines wanted to heat up the issue and sell some magazines." Ree steadfastly refused to comment to the press, and in a while the rumors died down.

But Aretha had another adversary to contend with. A new form of music called disco was quickly sweeping the nation and was making stars out of singers Donna Summer and Gloria Gaynor, and the group Village People. Disco was heard everywhere, and traditional rhythm and blues and soul artists were getting less play as a result. It was the disco albums that were selling, so it was the disco singles that got airplay.

After the disappointment of her fall 1975 release, *You*, which charted only one single, the Aretha-penned "Mr. D.J. (5 for the D.J.)," the staff at Atlantic sensed that it was time for another change for Aretha, who had once been their premier artist. Founder and cochairman Ahmet Ertegun presented Aretha with a list of its most popular producers to work with. She chose soul icon Curtis Mayfield, the former Impressions leader, who was at that time composing and producing movie soundtracks like *Superfly*. Mayfield, who was also steeped in the gospel tradition, agreed to collaborate with Aretha to produce and compose the soundtrack for the film *Sparkle*. Presenting the story of a female singing group attempting to achieve stardom and make it out of the ghetto, the film starred Irene Cara, who would go on to record the Oscar-winning themes to *Fame* and *Flashdance*. Aretha liked the story idea of some young sisters, possibly modeled after the Supremes, making their dreams come true through music.

Curtis Mayfield helped to compose and produce the soundtrack to the 1976 film Sparkle. *The album was a huge success for both Mayfield and Franklin.*

Aretha traveled to Chicago in January 1976 to record the songs Curtis Mayfield had written for the film. Released the following May, the soundtrack was a smash, and in time the album would become one of Aretha's own favorites. The urban-flavored tracks seemed to harken back to Aretha's Atlantic glory days. "Look into Your Heart" made the R&B top 10, while "Something He Can Feel" became number one on the same chart in the spring of 1976 and a Top 40 single too.

Meanwhile, Ken and Aretha were having some difficulties in their relationship. He had made some comments about Cecil Franklin's handling of some of Aretha's business affairs, and Aretha, always a defender of family members, took offense. Things were later smoothed over, but Aretha got to thinking about the relationship. With exciting things happening on the West Coast and their relationship in the doldrums, it seemed that a change might do them good.

In 1976, Aretha, Ken, and the children moved to Encino, in California's San Fernando Valley, into a house next to the Walt Disney mansion. There Clarence, Eddie, Teddy, and Kecalf made friends with some of their neighbors, who included Michael Jackson and his sister Janet.

The move to California presented Aretha with ample opportunities to heighten her profile after the warm reception to *Sparkle*. She made appearances on the most popular TV programs of the mid-1970s, including the *Dinah Shore Show*, *Tonight Show*, and *Hollywood Squares*, as well as specials hosted by Bob Hope and Muhammad Ali. In 1976 Aretha was asked to cohost the Grammy Awards show, a fitting tribute to one of the most honored women in Grammy history. The Queen of Soul made a warm and witty appearance.

That same year Aretha was given an honorary degree by Bethune-Cookman College in Jacksonville, Florida. This event was especially meaningful for Aretha, who had never graduated from high school. She felt great satisfaction to be associated with a college that had been founded by an African American, Mary McLeod Bethune, in the early 1900s, a time when it was unheard of for black people to go to college.

In her spare time Aretha kept up with several soap operas that she'd been watching for years, developed her interest in astrology, and watched and attended boxing matches with Ken (something she had done with her father since she was a girl). She also designed a rose-lined walkway that led from the street to her front door and cultivated her gardens.

By the mid-1970s, a few years into her relationship with Ken Cunningham, Aretha had gained back some of the weight she lost after her divorce from Ted

In 1976 Bethune-Cookman College, founded by educator Mary McLeod Bethune (front, center), honored Aretha with a degree.

White. Although Aretha did not think her weight was a problem, she was proved wrong while performing in Pittsburgh, Pennsylvania. Becoming short of breath during the concert, she knew a change in her habits was in the offing. She contacted the New York Academy of Ballet and asked the school to recommend someone she could work out with in the Los Angeles area. Thereafter, Aretha made ballet classes a regular part of her exercise regimen. She also tried several fad diets, losing about 40 pounds in four months.

At the beginning of 1977, things had come to a head in Aretha and Ken's disagreements over Cecil's business skills, ultimately dooming the relationship. The fact that Ken preferred New York to Los Angeles didn't help. The couple broke off their relationship, but Aretha and Ken maintained a cordial relationship. Cunningham headed back to the East Coast.

After the breakup with Ken Aretha recorded the album *Sweet Passion*. Calling in some new producers, arrangers, and writers, she worked with some of the best in the business, including the team of Marvin Hamlisch and Carole Bayer Sager. She also called on the talents of Lamont Dozier of the illustrious Holland-Dozier-Holland team, which had helped make so many Motown acts household names. The single written by Hamlisch and Bayer Sager, "Break It to Me Gently," went to number one on the R&B charts in the spring of 1977, but the overall response was disappointing.

In 1976 Aretha again performed at the Academy Awards, where she was so happy to see her father that she burst into tears. It had been over a year since they were last together. She also sang at President Jimmy Carter's pre-inaugural gala in January 1977, where Reverend Franklin again joined her.

Aretha dissolved her longtime business relationship with her booking agency that year during negotiations for her proposed tour of Britain. It had committed Aretha, who for years had kept a strict touring schedule to keep her voice in the right condition, to one too many dates. When the deal fell apart, Aretha was sued by the British concert promoter. Thereafter, she signed with International Creative Management (ICM), which snagged Aretha profitable deals singing in television commercials for products such as Armour hot dogs, Dial soap, and the Yellow Pages.

In 1977 Aretha contributed a performance at a charity benefit called Giant Step that was hosted by pro football star Rosey Grier. Aretha had brought her son Clarence with her. While she relaxed in her dressing room, Clarence scoured the high-profile crowd for autographs. Happening upon a handsome, thin black man in a cowboy hat, Clarence spoke with the man, who it turned out was an actor named Glynn Turman. Clarence brought Turman to Aretha's dressing room, where the two complimented each other's work and exchanged other pleasantries and phone numbers. Soon they began dating and seeing each other regularly.

Glynn Turman, also divorced, was a father of two boys and a girl and lived fairly close to Aretha. He had acted in the films *Cooley High* and *Five on the Black Hand Side*. An actor who was very serious about his craft, Turman was also known for his roles on the stage and for the acting classes he taught.

While accompanying Glynn to Texas, where he was starring in a play, Aretha was shocked when he proposed marriage. She accepted and began making preparations for a wedding very much unlike her first one.

Glynn Turman, seen here relaxing with Aretha, was known in entertainment for his performances in a variety of films. The two were married in April of 1978.

Rev. C. L. Franklin would be officiating at this wedding, the couple decided, and they would wed at the New Bethel Baptist Church in Detroit. The following day there would be a reception in Beverly Hills for their famous friends. In addition, this time there would be a prenuptial agreement, stating that what each had earned before the marriage would remain that person's property.

Two days before Aretha's 18th Atlantic album, *Almighty Fire*, was released, she and Glynn married. It was April 11, 1978, and crowds of fans flocked to see one of Detroit's most famous daughters wed the Hollywood actor. The bride wore a silk gown lined in mink fur, covered with thousands of small pearls, which had an eight-foot train attached to it. She was attended by eight bridesmaids, including her sister

Erma, who was the maid of honor. Among Glynn's eight groomsmen was the well-known actor Louis Gossett Jr., who was the best man. The Four Tops crooned the Stevie Wonder song "Isn't She Lovely" as Aretha entered the church, and Carolyn Franklin sang a song she had written for the occasion, "I Take This Walk with Thee."

All of the Franklin and Turman families were accounted for, too, as were journalists and photographers from national magazines clamoring for pictures of the happy couple as they left the New Bethel Baptist Church. Afterward, the dozens of guests celebrated by enjoying an eight-foot, four-tier wedding cake.

Although Aretha's personal life was certainly on the upswing, her career continued to flounder. *Almighty Fire*, which was her second project with Curtis Mayfield, stalled on the charts. A 1979 album, *La Diva*, was an even bigger disappointment. Only her live performances continued to inspire awe in critics and fans alike.

Aretha switched from ICM to the William Morris Agency, one of the most prestigious and long-lived of the Hollywood management companies. She also began to pursue other career options. Although Ahmet Ertegun (who was Aretha's main contact since Jerry Wexler's departure from Atlantic in the 1970s) offered to renew her contract at his label, Aretha and Cecil looked at other labels too, especially Arista Records. By 1976 much of Atlantic's stable of soul performers had left as the company switched its emphasis to rock acts; the holdouts at this point were Aretha, the Spinners, and Roberta Flack.

Arista was headed by Clive Davis, who had also worked at Columbia, Aretha's first pop label. Aretha, an avid reader of industry magazines like *Variety* and *Billboard*, had noticed that some of the most successful artists of the late 1970s were Arista acts. Vocalists like Melissa Manchester and Barry Manilow were both making huge hits under the promotional push provided by Arista and Clive Davis. Dionne Warwick, who had also had a lull in record sales, signed with the label and her album *Dionne* became one of the biggest sellers of her long career.

Aretha liked what she saw with regard to Davis, and they met to discuss a possible move to Arista. Davis very much wanted to sign Aretha, and she was looking for a label that could breathe life into a career that had stalled as the success of disco took off.

Meanwhile, Aretha appeared in another medium for the first time. Although she had been interested in acting since the early part of the decade, she had only received offers to play roles that she felt were too stereotypical for a black woman—the part of a maid or a sassy best friend. She had turned them all down.

In 1979 Aretha was offered a role in *The Blues Brothers*, a movie that starred Dan Aykroyd and John Belushi. She accepted the part of a no-nonsense soul food restaurant owner/waitress whose man leaves her to go on the road with the Blues Brothers Band. In the film, Aretha's character warns her husband to "think" about whether he should go on the road—at which point she sings a memorable up-tempo remake of the smash Aretha Franklin song "Think." Aretha's sisters Erma and Carolyn and her cousin Brenda provided backup vocals in the scene, and Aretha looked every bit the part of her character, wearing a stained apron, comfortable slippers, and a red tint to her hair. A who's who of soul, jazz, and R&B rounded out the cast of the movie, which included Cab Calloway, Ray Charles, John Lee Hooker, and James Brown.

In this 1981 photograph, Aretha performs at a piano under the attentive eye of Clive Davis, head of Arista Records.

When *The Blues Brothers* was released in 1980, it was a huge hit, and the soundtrack was soon certified gold. Aretha, who had attended some acting classes taught by her husband, was thrilled with the end result. Although some film critics didn't like *The Blues Brothers*, nearly everyone liked Aretha Franklin's performance in the musical comedy, calling her showstopping tune one of the best parts in the movie. Ree was also glad that audiences that were not familiar with her became fans as a result of the movie.

But before the release of the film, the entire Franklin family had to deal with enormous tragedy. On June 10, 1979, Aretha was performing at the Aladdin Hotel in Las Vegas. Coming offstage, she was met by Glynn and Cecil, who told his sister the bad news: their father had been shot during a robbery. Aretha was devastated, as was the entire family.

According to a report in the *Detroit Free Press*, the robbers had gone to the Franklin home in Detroit to steal an antique stained glass window. It seemed that during the robbery, Reverend Franklin had surprised the intruders and been shot twice, once in the groin and once in the knee. Some neighbors heard the shots, found the minister unconscious, and called an ambulance.

Reverend Franklin had fallen into a coma, albeit a light coma, since he needed no machines to keep him alive. Although the family was told that C. L.'s condition could change at any time, it didn't. He stayed in the coma for the next five years. While Carolyn, Cecil, and Erma Franklin took on the day-to-day duties of seeing to their father's care, Aretha commuted from her home in Encino to Detroit by plane twice a month. "A difficult chapter—perhaps the most difficult of my life—had opened," Aretha later wrote about this period. "Only my faith in God got me through."

Despite reports to the contrary, the men who robbed and shot Reverend Franklin were quickly captured, tried, and convicted. Although the family members were relieved by the arrests, their deepest concern was their father's health.

In the midst of her father's crisis, Aretha made the decision to leave Atlantic Records for Arista. Although it was a difficult decision to make, having had great success during the previous 12 years with Atlantic, Aretha felt the best place to be was under the guidance of Clive Davis.

7

THE ROAD BACK

❧

As ARETHA BEGAN the recording of her first album for Arista Records in 1980, her career was heating up again. She received positive reviews for her appearance in *The Blues Brothers*, and she was singled out as the Queen of Soul in the hit song "Hey Nineteen" by the rock band Steely Dan.

At Arista, Aretha appreciated Clive Davis's friendship, which reminded her of her relationship with Jerry Wexler. She liked the personal attention he was giving to her career and was happy that he trusted her skill, judgment, and experience in the studio.

The first Arista album was called simply *Aretha*. Aretha and Clive Davis had assembled for the album a team that included friends and professional contacts from her Atlantic days, including Cissy Houston and her Sweet Inspirations and Arif Mardin, who produced four songs for *Aretha*. Aretha played keyboards on some tracks, too, which brought back a little of the Atlantic flavor. The album featured a reworking of the Doobie Brothers' hit "What a Fool Believes," and a soaring ballad, "United Together." It was cowritten and produced by Chuck Jackson, who after working with Natalie Cole, had come into the Franklin fold.

"Can't Turn You Loose" was nominated for a Grammy, but Aretha did not win. The first Arista album was not a big hit, but its reception was encouraging nonetheless, and it kept Aretha fresh

As Aretha moved into the 1980s she continued to perform and saw a surge of success develop from her relationship with Arista Records.

in the minds of radio programmers and listeners alike.

Meanwhile, the vigil at the bedside of Reverend Franklin continued. Aretha and her siblings would sit for hours with C. L., hoping that he would show some sign of life. Although the Franklins were disappointed by the apparent indifference of some friends and parishioners to their father's tragedy and the incorrect reports by some local newspapers, they were heartened by the compassion of longtime ally Rev. Jesse Jackson and some other ministers with whom they were close.

Concerned about her father's mounting medical bills, Aretha continued to take gigs, playing venues like the Greek Theatre in Los Angeles. She also became involved in a dispute with Atlantic Records regarding some back royalties she felt she was owed. The company disagreed and at one point even publicly released some accounting statements pertaining to their former hitmaker in an attempt to demonstrate that Aretha was not owed anything.

After the release of *Aretha*, Lady Soul and her son Teddy headed to England for a tour. Although she had some concerns about committing to an overseas tour, remembering the problems she had had with her former booking agency, there was no need to worry. The British welcomed Aretha with open arms, and the tour was a great success.

"The opening date was the most spectacular. Sammy Davis, Jr., was the host of a gala command performance in London attended by Prince Charles and the Queen Mother. It was a moving night," Aretha remembered almost 20 years later. "I could hear the words my father had spoken to me when I was a child: 'One day you will sing for kings and queens.' That day had arrived."

Upon returning to the States, Aretha, working again with Arif Mardin, recorded her second album for Arista, *Love All the Hurt Away*. She wrote

the title song, a duet with singer/musician George Benson, and another, "Whole Lot of Me." Aretha also recorded "It's My Turn," which had been a hit for Diana Ross, and "Hold On, I'm Comin'," the old Sam & Dave 1960s gem. Aretha, who also co-produced the album, won her 11th Grammy, her first in seven years, for "Hold On, I'm Comin'."

Outside the studio, Aretha stayed busy with charity work and other interests. She established the Aretha Franklin Artist Ball, a fundraising event that benefitted the Sickle-Cell Anemia Foundation and the Arthritis Foundation. She also appeared in television commercials promoting the National Association for the Advancement of Colored People (NAACP).

Although seen here smiling together, the working relationship between Aretha and Luther Vandross was often a bumpy one.

Aretha displays her American Music Award for Best Soul Album, won for her work on the 1982 album Jump to It.

In 1981, joined by her husband, Glynn Turman, and their blended family, Aretha was honored with a star on the Hollywood Walk of Fame. Reflecting on her father and how proud he would have been to witness the occasion, Aretha was overcome with emotion at the ceremony.

While Clive Davis and Aretha were encouraged by the minor successes of her first two albums for Arista, they knew that it was time for a new strategy and that Aretha was capable of the hit records they both desired. Hearing that Luther Vandross, an up-and-coming singer and producer, had always wanted to work with the Queen of Soul, Davis contacted him. Vandross was quickly signed with partner Marcus Miller to produce Aretha's next album.

In early 1982 the team recorded *Jump to It* at Media Sound Studios in New York City. Upon release later in the year, the collaboration became a smash. *Jump to It* was Aretha's first gold album and her first number one album for Arista. The title track, in which Aretha and a pal named Kitty gossip about "who drop-kicked who" was one of the most successful songs of the summer of 1982 and Aretha's most successful in several years. It was a number one R&B single and did well on the pop charts, too. The following year, she was awarded the Best Soul Album trophy at the American Music Awards.

Despite this upswing in her professional life, Aretha was experiencing problems in her personal life. A distance had been steadily developing between her and Glynn as they spent longer periods of time apart because of Aretha's performance schedule and visits to Reverend Franklin, who remained in a coma back in Detroit. The problems became too much for the couple and they agreed to separate. In 1982, with her sons in tow, Aretha moved back to Detroit, where she could more easily be by her father's side. Glynn, still legally married to Aretha, stayed in California.

Before Aretha headed back to Michigan, a local politician arranged a special goodbye concert for her that was attended by close friends Smokey Robinson, Dionne Warwick, Luther Vandross, and up-and-coming singer Deniece Williams. The Queen was truly touched and appreciative.

After arriving back in her hometown, Aretha settled into the old Franklin family homestead, where she shared her old bedroom with her sister Carolyn. "I knew [Detroit] was where I belonged," Aretha wrote about her move. "Though he couldn't express it, though his condition didn't—and wouldn't—change, I felt my dad was comforted by our presence. Somehow, some way, I felt he knew we were there."

Getting on with business as usual after the move back to Detroit, Aretha returned to New York to record the follow-up to *Jump to It*. Again, Luther Vandross served as her producer, as Clive Davis and Aretha hoped to repeat the success of *Jump to It*. Unfortunately, that experience could not be duplicated, as problems developed between Aretha and

Luther Vandross. Aretha objected to Luther telling her how to sing certain songs, rather than just directing her phrasing and rhythmic patterns. A nasty argument between singer and producer ensued, with Aretha picking up her fur coat and walking out of the recording session. Deciding not to leave New York that night, Aretha returned to her hotel with plans to leave the following day.

Before Aretha left, however, Clive Davis was able to smooth things over and get the two temperamental talents to continue recording the album, which would be called *Get It Right*. The finished product included the track "Giving In," which was written by Aretha's son Clarence and featured guitar work by Teddy White. Although the album was not as big a success as the team's first effort, it sold a respectable number of copies and reached the number one position on the soul charts.

Now that Aretha was living full-time in Michigan and Glynn Turman was back on the West Coast, it seemed a more permanent separation was the next logical step for the estranged couple. Unlike her first divorce, this one was amicable. The prenuptial agreement took care of the financial and property concerns, and the couple kept silent about the reasons for their split, rather than making them public. Glynn stayed in the Los Angeles area, where he founded a ranch for needy children and later took a role in the *Cosby Show* spin-off *A Different World* (for which, coincidentally, Aretha would eventually sing the theme song, beginning in 1988).

In the early 1980s Aretha decided to try to deal with some phobias she had developed. Long afraid of heights—a fear that had been documented years earlier in New York City newspapers when she failed to show up for a reception held in her honor atop a skyscraper—Aretha had developed a new fear: flying. The phobia developed in 1983, during a flight from Atlanta back to Detroit. When the small plane she was traveling in experienced turbulence and made dramatic dips in the air, Aretha experienced an anxiety attack, although the plane eventually landed safely. Once back on solid ground, she jokingly told her road manager, "You don't have to worry about getting me on another plane soon." She did, however, believe she would in time be an air passenger again, but she did not attempt to conquer her phobia right away.

When a Broadway producer approached Aretha about the possiblity of playing Mahalia Jackson in a stage musical, Aretha expressed interest. *Sing, Mahalia, Sing* had the potential to open up creative doors for the singer, and she knew it. She signed the contracts and began learning the show's songs. Ultimately, however, Aretha decided that she would not be able to fly to New York for rehearsals because she could not conquer her fear of flying. A road trip to New York was aborted, too, and Aretha backed out of the deal.

The producer of the play later sued Aretha, and she was reportedly forced to pay $230,000 in damages to him. The Queen of Soul was apparently not meant to play the Queen of Gospel.

In the years that followed, Aretha attempted to overcome her fear, even going so far as to take US Airways' Fearful Flyers course. Unfortunately, she missed the last few sessions of the program and did not go on an actual flight with the other participants. As a result, Aretha's phobia still exists, and she has had to turn down performance offers throughout the world. Nevertheless she remains optimistic and insists that one day she will get the better of her fear.

In the meantime, Aretha purchased a large touring bus, which enabled her to get to the venues she plays. According to the star, the custom bus, called "The Legend," contains all the amenities of home— including a VCR, a small kitchen, a telephone, and a superior stereo unit.

In 1984, a sad day came to pass for the Franklin family. Rev. C. L. Franklin died on July 27, five years after falling into a coma. With his death, the family felt both enormous sadness and profound relief. "The suffering was over," Aretha later wrote. "The agonizing decisions that we had been forced to make were now behind us."

An estimated 10,000 mourners from the Motor City and all over the country passed through New Bethel Baptist Church to say their last good-byes to one of the city's most notable clergymen. *Newsweek* covered the story in an article that praised Reverend Franklin's stature and his accomplishments, among them, the 1963 Detroit march staged with Martin Luther King Jr. Aretha and the entire Franklin family would be deeply affected by Reverend Franklin's death.

That same year, the music world and soul music in particular lost two of its greatest stars, Marvin Gaye and Jackie Wilson. Aretha had been friendly with both men and had toured with Wilson when she first became famous. She now had to deal with the shock and grief of their deaths.

After taking most of 1984 off, the Queen of Soul returned to the studio—this time a hometown studio. "I liked the idea of recording close to home, and since producers and duet partners were willing to come to Detroit, the city became the center of my recording life," she wrote in *Aretha: From These Roots*. "They say there's no arguing with success, so I'm not arguing. Detroit has been good to me."

Not only did Ree have a new recording home-base, she also had a new producer—Narada (pronounced "Narda") Michael Walden, himself a recording artist, drummer, and songwriter. The astrology-minded Aretha expressed a bit of surprise that she and Walden, both Aries, could actually collaborate. Walden was honored and thrilled to work with the legendary diva. He recalled how pleased he was by her reaction to the material he penned for her: "She was delighted with what she heard. I sent

her [demos] on 'Push,' 'Freeway of Love,' and 'Who's Zoomin' Who.' I really came up with a lot of the ideas lyrically from talking with Aretha on the phone. . . . She told me that one of the things she liked to do on occasion was go to a club and maybe she'd be checking out some guy who'd be checking her out too—that's where I got a lot of the ideas for 'Who's Zoomin' Who.' I discovered that Aretha had this great sense of humor, something I had no idea about before we started working together."

Aretha usually arrived at the recording facility in a chauffer-driven limousine, wearing a long fur coat over sweats or a T-shirt and jeans. Walden and Ree got along famously in the studio and passed the time between songs by eating spareribs and joking around with each other. There were none of the ego problems that had plagued the recording of *Get It Right*.

Aretha offered her own opinion about the album *Who's Zoomin' Who?* just before its release in 1985: "I had decided I wanted to do a record that had a younger sound to it. I had been listening to some of the music on the radio and I really liked what I

During the 1980s, Aretha took time to collaborate with some of music's more popular acts, such as the Eurythmics, above.

heard. Records by Eurythmics, John Waite, Van Halen, the Stones, as well as Tina [Turner], Lionel [Richie], and Luther [Vandross]. . . . I wanted to do something for the kids. . . . I think it's some of the best material I've done since the mid-'60s!"

Who's Zoomin' Who? certainly sold like one of Aretha's 1960s classics. "Freeway of Love" was a number one R&B track and a number three single on the pop side of the *Billboard* charts. The video, showcasing the Motor City and a brassy Aretha in the pink cadillac featured in the song, played regularly on MTV. The title tune, which referred to one person's fooling—or thinking they're fooling—a lover, was another smash.

"Sisters Are Doin' It for Themselves" was a feminist anthem on which Aretha shared singing duty with Annie Lennox of the Eurythmics; like many songs on the album, it was a hit in dance clubs all over the country. The infectious track gave Aretha some extra street appeal with younger listeners, since the Eurythmics were considered to have a very edgy, hip sound. Other standouts on the album included "Sweet Bitter Love," a composition that Aretha had recorded two decades before, this time with a string arrangement, and the rock-oriented "Another Night," which spent seven weeks in the Top 40.

Aretha Franklin's first platinum album for Arista Records, *Who's Zoomin' Who?* was second only in sales figures to her Atlantic gospel recording *Amazing Grace. Zoomin'* was the crossover hit that both she and Clive Davis had anticipated when she signed with the label.

With Aretha's newest success came more accolades, including another Grammy statuette for "Freeway of Love," stellar reviews, and honors from her home state. On May 23, 1985, Michigan declared Lady Soul's voice "a natural resource" during what was proclaimed "Aretha Franklin Appreciation Day." In July of that year a section of Washington Boule-

vard in Detroit was renamed Aretha Franklin's Freeway of Love, and the following month, a portion of
Linwood Boulevard, home to New Bethel, had its
name changed to C. L. Franklin Boulevard.

Perhaps *Newsweek* best summed up that banner
year for Aretha in its review of *Who's Zoomin' Who?*
"Above all, there's that voice. It flutters and floats,
snaps and shouts, cries and laughs. Welcome back,
'Lady Soul.'"

8

WHAT YOU SEE IS WHAT YOU SWEAT

SINCE HER DIVORCE from Glynn, Aretha was playing the field, though she wasn't always happy with what she found out in the dating world: "I've met my share of guys between the ages of thirty and forty-five who have insulted and assaulted my intelligence with their stories and their games. When I met those kind of guys I say hello and *goodbye!* I like a man who can rise to the occasion!" She admitted that she wasn't thinking about getting remarried, but she also would never say never to that proposition, should it arise again.

Aretha moved a couple of times after her father's death and eventually settled in Bloomfield Hills, an affluent suburb just outside Detroit. Her six-bedroom colonial sits on three acres of land, with an inground swimming pool and lavish flower gardens. During her downtime, Ree spent time planting and cultivating a vegetable garden, reading, socializing with close friends, and cooking good old-fashioned soul food.

As Aretha was getting her new home in order, her lawyers and accountants were getting her finances and business in order. In 1985 the state of New York sued the superstar for more than $100,000 in back taxes it claimed she owed from her days recording there with Atlantic. Although Aretha was scheduled to perform at Carnegie Hall in the summer, she

Aretha performs at the opening of the Rock and Roll Hall of Fame in Cleveland, Ohio. In 1987, she became the first female performer to be inducted into the Hall of Fame.

canceled her concerts, either because of her over-whelming fear of flying or because the state would have a lien against the profits from the concert. The following year the suit was settled before it went to trial, but Aretha's reputation as a performer who can-celed dates grew.

With Narada Michael Walden at the producer's helm once again, Aretha's second self-titled album for Arista was recorded and released in 1986. Producer and performer had another smash hit to their credit with the milestone *Aretha*, which featured an Andy Warhol portrait of Lady Soul on its cover. Many of the album's brightest spots were numbers on which Aretha collaborated with other artists.

At the beginning of 1987, the album's duet with former Wham! member George Michael, "I Knew You Were Waiting (For Me)," took Aretha and Michael to the summit of the pop charts. The song was a hit internationally, and won the Grammy Award for Best R&B Performance by a Duo or Group with Vocal. "I Knew You Were Waiting," which spoke of finally finding the love of one's life, could have also been referring to Ree's successful quest to have another top pop single.

Aretha also recorded the classic Rolling Stones tune "Jumpin' Jack Flash" for the album and for the Whoopi Goldberg film of the same name. Rolling Stones members Keith Richards (lead guitar) and Ron Wood (guitar) joined the Queen on the song, which Richards also produced. Although the Stones' original version of the song remains hard to beat, Aretha and company breathed new life into the rocking tune. "Keith wanted me to play piano [on "Jumpin' Jack Flash"], and I hadn't done that in a long time," Aretha wrote years later.

The Grammy folks also favored the album, for which Aretha won "Best R&B Vocal Perform-ance" at the 30th annual ceremony, bringing her Grammy total to 14. Aretha did not attend the cere-

Aretha worked with singer George Michael in 1986. The following year, the two won a Grammy together for the hit single "I Knew You Were Waiting (For Me)."

mony. Instead, Cecil Franklin picked up the trophies for her.

Also in 1987, Aretha became the first woman to gain entrance to the elite Rock and Roll Hall of Fame, which was being built in Cleveland. A proud Aretha discussed this honor with a reporter from the *New York Daily News*, saying, "As far as getting into the Rock and Roll Hall of Fame, I have to say I never thought of myself as a rock 'n roll singer. But as they deal with people who are regarded as legendary or classic, it was certainly nice to be included."

One need only look at this honor to realize how far American society and American music had come in such a short time. Not only was Aretha Franklin the first woman to be inducted into the Hall of Fame, she was the first *black* woman. The country and the industry had made great strides in achieving racial equality since the 1950s, when black artists' records were separated from their white counterparts in catalogs and store shelves. Before the 1960s, pop music had been considered a white person's world.

Although thrilled with the success of her two Narada Michael Walden–produced pop albums, Aretha felt the need in late 1987 to again reconnect with her spiritual and musical roots. After many years of prompting from fans, she decided to make another gospel album, her first since *Amazing Grace* in 1972. Another reason for recording the album was Aretha's desire to honor her father's memory in the best way she knew how. She even recorded the album in her father's church in New Bethel. As a result the set of songs have a very familiar and sentimental quality.

In her 1999 autobiography, Aretha wrote at length about the experience of recording *One Lord, One Faith, One Baptism:* "When I think of those three magical nights in August, what stands out most is that we had a shouting good time and that old and new friends worshipped together. . . . Carolyn, Erma, cousin Brenda, and I were singing together for the first time in a very long time. Big Mama . . . was also with us. We didn't know the difficulties that would soon follow. . . . But for those three nights we were together as a family, singing and praying as we did as children. The spirits of our mom and dad were surely with us."

One Lord, One Faith, One Baptism was released in 1988 and was a minor success, but it gave Aretha a great sense of personal accomplishment. She had produced the album herself and had seen to many of the details of the three-night event, from the candlelight service, to the selection of hymns, to the presence of Jesse Jackson, to the blessing given by her brother Rev. Cecil Franklin.

There was a minor disagreement between Aretha and Mavis Staples over their recording of "Oh Happy Day." Staples accused Aretha the producer of "playing down" a portion Staples had sung so that Staples's voice didn't overshadow Franklin's. Aretha denied Mavis Staples's allegation, noting that "Mavis has a very *heavy* voice, and for us to sound equal, I had to put her just below me in the mix."

For *One Lord, One Faith, One Baptism*, Aretha was again recognized by her peers, winning the Grammy for Best Soul Gospel Performance, Female. Rev. Jesse Jackson was also presented a statuette for his spoken performance on the album. In 1988 the NAACP named Aretha Female Artist of the Year. PBS also aired an *American Masters* documentary, "Aretha Franklin—The Queen of Soul," highlighting Aretha's career.

It was during this period that the Franklin family again took center stage in Aretha's life. "It was the name of my last album of the eighties, but *Through the Storm* also described what my family was going through during that time," Aretha notes in *Aretha: From These Roots*.

On April 25, 1988, Carolyn Franklin, Aretha's younger sister and author of some of the Queen of Soul's most memorable songs, died of breast cancer. It had been diagnosed about a year earlier. While undergoing treatments Carolyn had attended Marygrove College. The degree she earned was awarded while she sat in bed, surrounded by her family. That night, Carolyn is said to have slept with her diploma.

The entire family was stunned and hurt by Carloyn's unexpected death. More sorrow was on the way. Just after Carolyn died, Cecil Franklin was diagnosed with lung cancer. Unfortunately, he was not able to win his battle with the disease, and he died on December 26, 1989. His funeral, like those of his father and sister, was held at New Bethel, the church to which the Franklins will be forever linked.

With Cecil gone, Aretha's other brother Vaughn Franklin took over the reins of road manager. A serviceman for many years, Vaughn agreed to help his sister and travel with her while she toured. Aretha also became more personally involved in the financial end of her business dealings as the 1980s wound down.

Released in 1989, *Through the Storm* was not a huge success for Aretha. She did have fun, though, recording several songs on the album on which she was paired with other legendary performers. Elton John joined her for the title track, which charted at number 16 on the pop list, while Godfather of Soul James Brown joined the Queen of Soul on "Gimme Your Love."

The album included a duet, "It Isn't, It Wasn't, It Ain't Never Gonna Be," with fellow Arista act Whitney Houston, who was one of the most popular singers around. Although the song received some airplay, it was not what would be called a "hit." Aretha was disappointed with the album's reception, including negative reviews from magazines like *Rolling Stone*. However, Aretha remains philosophical and grounded about the music world. "Artists have peaks and valleys . . . and I've been in the business long enough to know to go with the flow. No artist can produce a hit album every time out. If I was going into a quiet period, I could accept it."

Although *Through the Storm* was not a blockbuster, concerts kept Aretha busy as fans packed venues to see Lady Soul sing. For the first time in many years, Aretha played New York City, specifically Radio City Music Hall. David Nathan of *Blues & Soul* magazine witnessed the triumphant return, which included Aretha arriving onstage in a pink Cadillac (as in the "Freeway of Love" video) and per-

Aretha and James Brown collaborated together on the song "Gimme Your Love" for the 1989 album Through the Storm.

forming a couple of songs with Peabo Bryson. Even though Aretha had a cold at the time and couldn't reach some of the higher notes, the audience responded with enthusiasm.

The *New York Times* said of her three-night engagement at the legendary venue: "Aretha's voice is one of the glories of American music. . . . her singing melts down any divisions between gospel, soul, jazz and rock."

In December 1990 Aretha received a Grammy Legends Award, along with Johnny Cash, Billy Joel, and Quincy Jones. That year she also entertained at an event in honor of South African leader Nelson Mandela. In January 1991, she took part in a concert sponsored by the Congress of Racial Equality.

Having often won Grammy Awards for her work, Aretha received special recognition when honored with the Grammy Legends Award in 1991.

In 1991 *What You See Is What You Sweat*, Aretha's ninth Arista album, was dedicated by the singer to the two siblings she had recently lost. Included on the album were a reworking of Sly and the Family Stone's "Everyday People" (produced by Narada Michael Walden), the bittersweet Burt Bacharach/Carole Bayer Sager/Bill Conti ballad "Ever Changing Times" (with Michael McDonald also lending vocals), and "I Dreamed a Dream," a memorable tune from the Broadway musical *Les Miserables*. The album was also the first project to reteam Aretha and

Luther Vandross since the 1983 hit *Get It Right*. They sang on the duet "Doctor's Orders," and again there was friction in their working relationship. Aretha complained to Luther, who was also producer of the song, that he had her voice level too low in the mix. Finally, after much back and forth, the song was released in a remix that all found acceptable, but relations between the stars remained tense.

Although *What You See* didn't see much chart action, performing engagements followed at theaters in the Midwest and at Caesar's Palace in Las Vegas. Indeed, in the early 1990s Aretha told an interviewer that "Performing is something I never tire of. It's lost none of its magic for me." And her fans have never tired of seeing her perform.

9
THE REIGN CONTINUES

ALTHOUGH ARETHA WAS still cutting some great singles as the 1990s began, *Through the Storm* and *What You See Is What You Sweat* had failed to perform on the charts and in the stores. This hardly seemed to matter to the organizations that bestowed awards on performers or to the organizers of some high-profile events. In May 1992 Aretha received a Lifetime Achievement Award at the third annual Rhythm and Blues Foundation Pioneer Awards, an honor that must have meant a lot to the woman who began her secular career singing mostly jazz and blues standards.

In 1992 Aretha lent her vocal talents to *A Very Special Christmas 2*, an album of both new and traditional Christmas carols performed by various artists. Sales of the album helped raise funds for the Special Olympics. Backed by a full orchestra, Aretha arranged and sang a beautiful, standout version of "O Christmas Tree."

The Queen of Soul also took center stage in Washington, D.C., invited by President Bill Clinton to perform at two inaugural balls held in his honor in January 1993. Aretha participated in the televised inaugural gala, along with entertainers Barbra Streisand and Fleetwood Mac. Some would later claim that her rendition of "I Dreamed a Dream" was one of the best performances of her career.

Divas Live: The One and Only Aretha Franklin aired on cable music channel VH1 in April 2001. It was a fitting tribute to the Queen of Soul.

Aretha sang a stirring version of "I Dreamed a Dream" at the televised inaugural gala for President Clinton in 1993.

The spring of 1993 brought Aretha back to New York, where she performed at an AIDS benefit at the Nederlander Theater, joined by fellow vocalists Rod Stewart, Bonnie Raitt, Smokey Robinson, and Gloria Estefan. The one-of-a-kind performance, which featured the female singers giving a particularly soulful rendition of "(You Make Me Feel Like) A Natural Woman," was taped and later aired on the Fox television network as a special, entitled *Aretha Franklin: Duets*.

The Queen of Soul also received some negative publicity around this time. *People* magazine and some newspapers reported that a vacant house in Detroit that Aretha apparently owned was becoming an eyesore. There were also reports of trouble with the I.R.S. for not paying taxes. And critics ripped into Aretha on her choice of clothing every chance they got. One journalist said the fur Aretha wore to the inaugural gala "may stand as the Pearl Harbor of the animal-rights movement." Through it all Aretha strove to keep a low-key image, once even describing herself as "just the nice lady who lives next door."

It was in 1994 that Lady Soul returned to the charts, when Arista released *Greatest Hits (1980–1994)*, a compilation of the best material that Aretha had recorded for the label, including a few songs recorded especially for the new hits package.

Two of the new songs were big successes. "Willing to Forgive," which was cowritten and coproduced by Kenny "Babyface" Edmonds, was a hit in R&B circles and also received airplay on adult contemporary stations. "A Deeper Love," which also appeared on the soundtrack to *Sister Act 2: Back in the Habit*, entered the dance charts at number one its first week out. With its positive message of self-reliance and its steady pumping beat, it quickly became a staple in dance clubs. The song showed that "[Aretha still] has relevance," Clive Davis proudly commented in a 1995 Disney Channel special about Aretha.

The honors kept coming. In March 1994, the National Academy of Recording Arts and Sciences recognized Aretha one more time with its most prestigious prize—the coveted Lifetime Achievement Award. According to the academy's citation, she was honored "for bringing the passion of gospel into the secular realm with her incomparable, four-octave range, and unparalleled confluence of heart and soul." The declaration went on to say that "The Queen of Soul's powerful, transcendent recordings will continue to inspire the greatest artists of generations to come."

While accepting the Lifetime Achievement Award, Aretha later explained, she was overcome with emotion when thanking her deceased brother Cecil. She let a few unguarded tears flow but then quickly regained her composure and continued her acceptance speech.

The Queen of Soul returned to Washington to sing again for President and Mrs. Clinton that summer, this time in the intimate setting of the White House Rose Garden. She was joined by singer and friend Lou Rawls, Rev. Jesse Jackson, and Mayor Dennis Archer of Detroit. Wearing an elegant white silk dress covered with beads and pearls, Aretha rocked the garden in a musical journey that celebrated the roots of American music. From "Ol' Man River" to "Brand New Me" to "Tomorrowland" (from *An Affair to Remember,* one of her favorite films), the cheering White House audience felt the energy she expended in her performance on that hot June night. It was even reported that Aretha was so into the music at one point that she lost a shoe going from one end of the stage to the other.

The greatest of her many accolades was to come in December 1994 when Aretha Franklin became the youngest recipient up to that time to be selected for the Kennedy Center Honors, the annual award that recognizes excellence in artistic endeavors. Also receiving the prestigious award in the nation's capital that year were actor Kirk Douglas, folk musician Pete Seeger, theater director Harold Prince, and composer Morton Gould. Performing in honor of Aretha at the lavish ceremony were Patti LaBelle, the Four Tops, and the New Bethel Baptist Church choir.

Charitable activities have continued to occupy Aretha's time. Her Aretha Franklin Scholarship Awards are celebrated each year at a banquet at which minority students who have won the scholarships are entertained by famous acts. In the mid-1990s Aretha also contributed a song to the album *Women for Women*, which benefited breast cancer research, and she appeared on a telethon that raised funds for the United Negro College Fund.

A March 1994 *Vanity Fair* profile of Aretha seemed to cause the subject some pain. Among other things, the article claimed that Barbara Siggers Franklin, Aretha's mother, had mysteriously abandoned the family, when in fact Barbara and C. L. had simply separated. Some quotes attributed to singer Mavis Staples regarding their duet "Oh Happy Day" also upset Aretha. *Vanity Fair* also recounted the Queen of Soul's war of words with gossip columnist Liz Smith.

Negative remarks from Smith had appeared previously. In a column published after the AIDS benefit concert at the Nederlander Theatre, Smith had negatively critiqued Aretha's choice in apparel, writing, "She must know she's too bosomy to wear such clothing, but clearly she doesn't care what we think, and that attitude is what separates mere stars from true divas."

Aretha didn't let Smith's salvo be the last word on her fashion sense. She replied in a letter to Smith:

"How dare you be so presumptuous as to presume you could know my attitudes with respect to anything other than music. . . . When you get to be a noted and respected fashion editor, please let us all know." Despite some unflattering publicity, Aretha maintains that although she's had her run-ins with journalists, there are no hard feelings.

It certainly was not the first time Aretha's fashions had come under scrutiny. Nor was it the first time she was referred to as a diva, a term that comes from the Italian word for "goddess," but is usually meant to describe a prima donna, or vain and undisciplined person. In the 1990s the term became popular and took on new significance, usually describing a strong-willed female performer, usually a singer or actress, who has a reputation of being difficult to deal with on occasion.

Aretha continued to have a high-profile career in the 1990s. In 1994 she joined Patti LaBelle and Gladys Knight on *The Oprah Winfrey Show* to celebrate the host's 40th birthday. She could also be heard each week singing an "Aretha-ized" version of "Lady Madonna" over the credits of the hit TV comedy *Grace Under Fire*.

Aretha established her own recording label, World Class Records, and was looking into beginning a film production company, which she eventually christened Crown Productions. In December 1996 Aretha recorded a Christmas gospel concert at New Bethel for World Class with guests Vanessa Bell Armstrong and Billy Preston. She also performed and recorded at Carnegie Hall with Stephanie Mills. And in 1997, Lady Soul was the Mistress of Ceremonies at the Rhythm and Blues Pioneer Awards.

What would be a busy two-year period began in 1998 for Aretha. After taking to the screen again in *Blues Brothers 2000* to reprise her cameo role from *The Blues Brothers*, there were her two triumphant performances at the Grammys and the release of *A Rose Is Still a Rose*, her first album of new material in

Aretha raises her arms in jubilation following her last-minute stand-in performance of "Nessun dorma" for an ill Luciano Pavarotti at the 1998 Grammy Awards.

seven years. Aretha continued her tradition of working with the most innovative writers and producers. She also produced some of the album and penned the track "The Woman," which some considered one of the album's high points. Lauryn Hill, a singer with the hip-hop group the Fugees, who was about to have a megahit solo album of her own, wrote the title single and directed the video for it. The song was yet another R&B and pop benchmark in Aretha's career, and both the *Rose* album and single went gold.

Entertainment Weekly described the single: "When Lady Soul sings about a rose, something divine happens. Writer-producer Lauryn Hill . . . wisely provides Franklin with enough hip-hop momentum to lure the Puff Daddy crowd without catering to them. Even after a dozen listens, the song's it's-his-problem-not-yours message doesn't lose its bloom." The same publication also appreciated the album itself: "*Rose* . . . has an unusual bloom. On tunes like 'Every Lil' Bit Hurts' and 'Never Leave You Again,' coproducers Sean

'Puffy' Combs, Jermaine Dupri, Lauryn Hill and others help Franklin recapture a gutsy urgency long missing from her records, earning her r-e-s-p-e-c-t once more."

On April 14 in New York City, cable music channel VH1 invited Aretha and several other top female singers to participate in *Divas Live*, a televised benefit concert for VH1 Save the Music Foundation, a nonprofit organization that helps to fund music education in and supply musical instruments to public schools. Not only would Aretha be helping out a good cause, she would also be sharing the stage with fellow divas Mariah Carey, Gloria Estefan, Celine Dion, and others. Some of the women who shared the stage with Aretha that night had undoubtedly been influenced by her, especially Celine Dion and Carey. Mariah has noted in interviews that her childhood idols were Stevie Wonder and Aretha Franklin.

Mariah and Aretha shared the Beacon Theatre stage for a duet of "Chain of Fools," one of the most popular songs in Aretha's career, and the entire audience, which included Clive Davis and real estate millionaire Donald Trump, erupted in enthusiastic howls. Toward the end of the show, all five featured singers—Aretha Franklin, Mariah Carey, Shania Twain, Gloria Estefan, and Celine Dion—took the stage for a rollicking rendition of "(You Make Me Feel Like) A Natural Woman." Joining them at the piano in a musically historic moment was one of the cowriters of the song, singer Carole King. The divas ended the night on a gospel high note, with all of them joining in on a stomping-in-the-aisles version of "I've Got a Testimony."

Aretha closed out 1998 with three nights of concerts with the Detroit Symphony Orchestra, singing the gospel music of her childhood, the classics of her Atlantic heyday, her newer hits, and a few opera arias for good measure. Ree also made stops at two hospitals on New Year's Eve, where she entertained the patients.

The following year, Aretha surfaced in radio and TV commercials for Pepsi's "Joy of Cola" advertising campaign and as a nurse who discovers her true calling as a singer in a humorous television spot for Prodigy Internet. VH1 gave Aretha the top position in a special that aired in the summer of 1999, *100 Greatest Women in Rock & Roll*. The winners were picked by a panel of more than 300 prominent women, including actress Sandra Bullock, feminist Gloria Steinem, and designer Donatella Versace. Fellow singers Bonnie Raitt, Marianne Faithful, and Gloria Estefan heaped praise on Ree, with Faithful declaring, "The voice of God, if you want to know, is Aretha Franklin." The VH1 special pointed out that not only did Aretha have the most Grammy Awards of any woman in history, she also had more million-selling singles than any other female recording artist.

Aretha contributed vocals to the track "Don't Waste Your Time" on Mary J. Blige's 1999 release, *Mary*. Blige, Elton John, and others have been slated to join Aretha for her next album, an untitled project yet to be released. According to industry reports, the album will feature old favorites and some new material, but assembling all of the talent has been complex.

The public eye kept Aretha Franklin firmly in focus as her fourth decade as a singer came to a close. In the fall of 1999, her long-delayed autobiography, *Aretha: From These Roots*, a project that she and collaborator David Ritz had worked on for almost four years, was published. To promote the book, Ree appeared on *Entertainment Tonight* and *The Oprah Winfrey Show*, which devoted a wide-ranging hour to her.

Talking with Oprah Winfrey, Aretha was candid about her problems, saying that losing weight and raising her children have been her toughest tasks in life. She expressed her desire to marry again, saying, "I love being married. . . . I am definitely domestic," but she was coy when it came to naming the man she's presently seeing, just as she always has been about her private life." She revealed that had she not been a singer, she would have liked to have been a nurse like her mother or maybe a prima ballerina.

In December Aretha was a guest on the Christmas special *Martha Stewart's Home for the Holidays*, during which she shared the recipe for the traditional Franklin family baked ham. After displaying her prowess in the kitchen, she sang a beautifully interpreted version of "Silent Night."

During that same month, Aretha and fellow Arista perfomers Carly Simon, Whitney Houston, Kenny G, and others came out in support of label president Clive Davis. Executives at Arista's parent company, BMG Entertainment, were reportedly trying to oust Davis in favor of younger successor L. A. Reid.

Major recognition had come Aretha's way in September 1999 when President Bill Clinton bestowed upon her the National Medal of Arts. In January 2000, Aretha's recording of "Respect" was picked by 700 music industry insiders as the second greatest song in all of rock and roll, as compiled by VH1. The Rolling Stones' "(I Can't Get No) Satisfaction" took the top spot, and Led Zeppelin's opus "Stairway to Heaven" was number three. The Beatles, Bob Dylan, and Elvis Presley were among those keeping Aretha company on the list.

In April 2001 the cable music channel VH1 again saluted the Queen of Soul, this time in a special Divas concert dedicated just to her. *Divas Live: The One and Only Aretha Franklin* aired in honor of the legendary star in a live performance at New York City's Radio City Music Hall. The program featured hip-hop performer Mary J. Blige, rising star Jill Scott, salsa singers Celia Cruz and Marc Anthony, and rock artist Kid Rock. During the event Franklin sang a duet, "Precious Memories," with Pentecostal minister Paul H. Morton, as well as her old standards like "Respect" and "Freeway of Love."

A jubilant President Bill Clinton awards Aretha the National Medal of the Arts in 1999.

Aretha Franklin has big plans for the future. As of this writing she is studying opera with a voice coach. In 2001 she announced that she will cut an album of arias, including Puccini's "Nessun dorma," and that she will enroll at Juilliard, the famed New York performing arts school. "I want to improve my skills on the piano," she explained. "I realize that I have not given nearly as much time to the piano as I can. And I can play piano a lot better; I have just focused on my voice."

Other plans included writing a cookbook, establishing a chicken and waffles restaurant chain, and spending quality time with her children, grandchildren, and other loved ones. And, of course, music.

Anyone who has ever heard Aretha's voice instantly knows that it is *her* voice and *her* song that they are hearing. Her classic singles—"Respect,"

"Think," "Chain of Fools," and "Freeway of Love"—
have earned a permanent place in the annals of popular music. People the world over recognize Aretha—
no last name needed—and her influence can be heard
in the music of many younger artists.

There's no mistaking the sound of the Queen of
Soul. It was many years ago that Aretha Franklin
demanded and earned respect, and she's continued to
get respect every time she sings. "I'll never stop," she
has said. "There's always one more song to sing. I've
got a million songs to sing."

CHRONOLOGY

1942   Aretha Louise Franklin is born on March 25 in Memphis, Tennessee, to Rev. C. L. Franklin and Barbara Siggers Franklin

1944   Franklin family moves to Detroit, Michigan

1948   C. L. and Barbara Franklin separate; Barbara moves to Buffalo, New York, with son Vaughn

1952   Barbara Franklin dies of a heart attack in Buffalo; Aretha is baptized at New Bethel Baptist Church; sings her first solo there

1956–57   Son Clarence is born; Aretha leaves high school and tours with her father's Gospel Caravan; Chess Records releases *Songs of Faith*

1959   Son Edward is born

1960   Aretha signs with Columbia Records; releases her first secular album, *Aretha*

1961   Marries Ted White in Ohio

1964   Friend Sam Cooke dies; *Unforgettable: A Tribute to Dinah Washington* is released

c. 1965   Son Ted White Jr. is born

1966   Aretha leaves Columbia Records for Atlantic Records

1967   First Atlantic album, *I Never Loved a Man the Way I Love You*, is a smash; "Respect" goes to number one on the pop and R&B charts; wins Best Rhythm & Blues Solo Vocal Performance, Female, and Best Rhythm & Blues Recording Grammy Awards for "Respect"

1968   Sings at the Democratic National Convention in Chicago; is pictured on the cover of *Time* magazine and featured in the cover article about soul music; divorces Ted White; performs "Precious Lord, Take My Hand" at the funeral of Martin Luther King Jr.

1970   Son Kecalf is born to Aretha and Ken Cunningham

1972   Releases two milestone albums, *Young, Gifted and Black* and *Amazing Grace*; *Grace* becomes the best-selling gospel album of all time

1976   Ends relationship with Ken Cunningham; cohosts the Grammy Awards

1978   Marries actor Glynn Turman

1979	Leaves Atlantic Records for Arista Records; films first movie, *The Blues Brothers*; father, Rev. C. L. Franklin, is shot and falls into a coma
1980	*The Blues Brothers* is released; Aretha entertains members of England's royal family at a command performance
1982	*Jump to It*, first album recorded with producer Luther Vandross, is a hit; Aretha moves back to Detroit; she and Glynn Turman separate and eventually divorce
1983	Develops a fear of flying after a turbulent flight from Atlanta; buys a luxury touring bus
1984	Reverend Franklin dies five years after entering a coma
1985	Album *Who's Zoomin' Who?* is a smash on all music charts
1986	"I Knew You Were Waiting (For Me)," a duet with George Michael, becomes first number one pop single for Aretha in 19 years
1987	Becomes the first woman inducted into the Rock and Roll Hall of Fame; earns two more Grammys for 1986 album *Aretha*
1988	Earns 15th Grammy Award for gospel album *One Lord, One Faith, One Baptism*; sister Carolyn dies of breast cancer
1989	Brother Cecil dies of lung cancer; brother Vaughn takes over as road manager
1993	Performs at inaugural festivities for President Bill Clinton in January
1994	Receives Kennedy Center Honors award for lifetime achievement in the performing arts; also is granted the Lifetime Achievement Grammy Award
1998	*A Rose Is Still a Rose* is released to critical and commercial success; *Blues Brothers 2000* is released; is named to the "*Time* 100" list of top artists and entertainers of the 20th century
1999	Autobiography, *Aretha: From These Roots*, is published; appears in a series of radio and TV commercials; receives National Medal of Arts from President Bill Clinton
2000	"Respect" is named the second-greatest rock song of all time in a VH1 poll
2001	Recognized by VH1 in *Divas Live: The One and Only Aretha Franklin* program

SELECTED DISCOGRAPHY

Chess Records

1956   *Songs of Faith* (reissued in 1967 as *The Gospel Soul of Aretha Franklin* and again in 1982 as *Aretha Gospel*)

Columbia Records

1960   *Aretha* (reissued in 1972 as *The Great Aretha Franklin—The First 12 Sides*)

1962   *The Electrifying Aretha Franklin*

1963   *Laughing on the Outside*

1964   *Runnin' Out of Fools*

           Unforgettable: A Tribute to Dinah Washington

1965   *Yeah!*

1966   *Soul Sister*

Atlantic Records

1967   *I Never Loved a Man the Way I Love You*

           Aretha Arrives

1968   *Lady Soul*

           Aretha Now

           Aretha in Paris

1969   *Aretha Franklin: Soul '69*

1970   *This Girl's in Love with You*

           Spirit in the Dark

1971   *Live at Fillmore West*

1972   *Young, Gifted and Black*

           Amazing Grace (reissued in 1999 by Rhino as *Amazing Grace: The Complete Recordings*)

1973   *Hey Now Hey (The Other Side of the Sky)*

1974   *Let Me in Your Life*

           With Everything I Feel in Me

1975	*You*
1976	*Sparkle: Music from the Warner Bros. Motion Picture*
1977	*Sweet Passion*
1978	*Almighty Fire*
1979	*La Diva*

Arista Records

1980	*Aretha*
1981	*Love All the Hurt Away*
1982	*Jump to It*
1983	*Get It Right*
1985	*Who's Zoomin' Who?*
1986	*Aretha*
1988	*One Lord, One Faith, One Baptism*
1989	*Through the Storm*
1991	*What You See Is What You Sweat*
1994	*Greatest Hits (1980–1994)*
1998	*A Rose Is Still a Rose*

Compilations and Soundtracks

1980	*The Blues Brothers* (soundtrack contribution)
1984	*The Best of Aretha Franklin* (Atlantic)
1986	*30 Greatest Hits* (Atlantic)
1992	*A Very Special Christmas 2* (song contribution; A&M Records)
	Aretha Franklin—The Queen of Soul: The Atlantic Recordings (Atlantic/Rhino; boxed set)
1994	*Miracle on 34th Street* (soundtrack contribution)
1998	*Blues Brothers 2000* (soundtrack contribution)

GRAMMY AWARDS

Awarded on an annual basis by the National Academy of Recording Arts and Sciences, the Grammy Award represents one of the highest honors in the music industry.

Year	Title of Work	Award
1967	"Respect"	Best R&B Recording
	"Respect"	Best R&B Solo Vocal Performance, Female
1968	"Chain of Fools"	Best R&B Vocal Performance, Female
1969	"Share Your Love with Me"	Best R&B Vocal Performance, Female
1970	"Don't Play That Song"	Best R&B Vocal Performance, Female
1971	"Bridge Over Troubled Water"	Best R&B Vocal Performance, Female
1972	*Amazing Grace*	Best Soul Gospel Performance
	Young, Gifted and Black	Best R&B Vocal Performance, Female
1973	"Master of Eyes"	Best R&B Vocal Performance, Female
1974	"Ain't Nothing Like the Real Thing"	Best R&B Vocal Performance, Female
1981	"Freeway of Love"	Best R&B Vocal Performance, Female
1981	"Hold On I'm Comin'"	Best R&B Vocal Performance, Female
1987	"I Knew You Were Waiting (For Me)" (with George Michael)	Best R&B Performance by a Duo or Group with Vocal
1987	*Aretha*	Best R&B Vocal Performance, Female
1988	*One Lord, One Faith, One Baptism*	Best Soul Gospel Performance, Female
1990	Grammy Legends Award	
1994	Grammy Lifetime Achievement Award	

FURTHER READING

Books

Boyer, Horace Clarence, and Lloyd Yearwood. *How Sweet the Sound: The Golden Age of Gospel*. Montgomery, Ala.: Black Belt Communications Group, 1995.

Dolan, Sean. *Pursuing the Dream: From the Selma-Montgomery March to the Foundation of PUSH*. Philadelphia: Chelsea House, 1995.

Franklin, Aretha, and David Ritz. *Aretha: From These Roots*. New York: Villard, 1999.

Nathan, David. *The Soulful Divas: Personal Portraits of Over a Dozen Divine Divas, from Nina Simone, Aretha Franklin, and Diana Ross, to Patti LaBelle, Whitney Houston, and Janet Jackson*. New York: Billboard Books, 1999.

Smith, Suzanne E. *Dancing in the Street: Motown and the Cultural Politics of Detroit*. Cambridge, Mass.: Harvard University Press, 1999.

Werner, Craig Hansen. *A Change Is Gonna Come: Music, Race, and the Soul of America*. New York: Dutton/Plume, 1999.

Websites

Arista Records: Aretha Franklin
http://www.aristarec.com/aristaweb/ArethaFranklin/

Mr. Showbiz: Aretha Franklin
http://mrshowbiz.go.com/people/arethafranklin/index.html

Rock and Roll Hall of Fame: Aretha Franklin
http://mrshowbiz.go.com/people/arethafranklin/index.html

INDEX

A
Ali, Muhammad, 60
Allman, Duane, 44
Alpert, Herb, 48
American Bandstand, 33
Archer, Mayor Dennis, 93
Aretha Franklin: Duets, 92
"Aretha Franklin: Queen of Soul," documentary, 14, 20
Aretha: From These Roots, 13, 19, 75, 85, 98
Arista Records, 64, 65, 67, 69, 71, 78, 86, 88, 99
Armstrong, Vanessa Bell, 95
Ashford, Nickolas, 55
Atlantic Records, 37–38, 48, 49, 53, 55, 57, 59, 70
Aykroyd, Dan, 12, 65

B
Bacharach, Burt, 88
Basie, Count, 28
Beatles, 31, 48, 52, 99
Belushi, John, 65
Benson, George, 70–71
Bethune-Cookman College, 60
Bethune, Mary McLeod, 60
Bishop, Louise, 37
Blues & Soul magazine, 86
Blues Brothers, The, 12, 65–66, 69, 95
Breakfast at Tiffany's, 33
Brown, James, 65, 86
Brown, Ruth, 37
Bryson, Peabo, 87

C
Calloway, Cab, 65
Capitol Records, 58
Cara, Irene, 59
Carter, President Jimmy, 62
Cash, Johnny, 87
Cavanaugh, Mayor James, 43
Charles, Ray, 37, 50–51, 65
Chess Records, 23, 24
Civil rights movement, 24, 25,

33. *See also* King, Reverend Martin Luther, Jr.
"Respect," as rallying cry for, 40–41
strides made from, 84
Clapton, Eric, 44
Cleveland, Reverend James, 24, 52–53
Clinton, President Bill, 91, 93
Cole, Natalie, 21, 57–58, 69
Cole, Nat "King," 18, 57
Cole, Paula, 12–13
Columbia Records, 27–28, 29, 30, 31, 32, 35
Combs, Sean "Puffy," 14, 97
Congress of Racial Equality, 87
Conti, Bill, 88
Cooke, Sam, 18, 21, 25, 28, 29, 44
death of, 34–35
Cooley High, 63
Corbett, Brenda, 42, 65
Cunningham, Ken E. (Wolf), 47–48, 49, 50, 61–62

D
Davis, Clive, 64–65, 67, 69, 71, 73, 78, 93, 97, 99
Davis, Miles, 29
Davis, Sammy, Jr., 70
Detroit, 18–19, 25, 72, 76, 79, 81
Diddley, Bo, 23
Different World, A, 73
Dinah Shore Show, 60
Disco, 58
Doobie Brothers, 69
Dowd, Tom, 40
Dozier, Lamont, 62
Drifters, 38
Dupri, Jermaine, 14, 97

E
Edmonds, Kenny "Babyface," 92
Ed Sullivan Show, The 32
Edwards, Bernard, 58

Edwards, Dennis, 47
Emancipation Proclamation, 24
Ertegun, Ahmet, 49, 59, 64
Eurythmics, 78

F
Fame, 59
Fame Studios, 38, 39
Five on the Black Hand, 63
Flack, Roberta, 64
Flashdance, 59
Fleetwood Mac, 91
Four Tops, 31, 64
Franklin, Aretha
AIDS benefit, 92
appears on Martha Stewart special, 99
Aretha Franklin Scholarship Awards, 94
awards and honors accorded to, 41, 43, 44–45, 48, 51, 53, 55, 58, 60, 62, 71, 72, 78, 82, 83, 84, 85, 87, 91, 93, 94, 95, 99
bad publicity of, 92
becomes more involved in civil rights struggle, 34
charity work of, 62, 71, 94
children of, 22, 25, 30, 49
critics take notice of, 29
decides on pop music career, 25, 27, 28
Detroit childhood of, 18–21
develops phobias, 11, 73–74, 80
Divas Live, 97
downturn in career of, 57–59
entertains at presidential events, 91, 93
establishes World Class Records, 95
fashion statements of, 55, 92, 94–95
first million-selling record of, 40

first woman in Rock and Roll
Hall of Fame, 83
friendship of Sam Cooke and,
21–22, 28, 29, 34–35
future plans of, 100
gets finances and business in
order, 80
increasing popularity of, 33
Lifetime Achievement Award,
93
men in life of. *See* Cunningham, Ken E.; Turman,
Glynn; White, Ted
moves back to Detroit area,
81
performs in *The Blues Brothers*,
65–66
recording contracts of. *See*
specific record companies
royalty attends command
performance of, 70
sings in honor of Pavarotti, 11
Special Olympics, 91
"The Legend," custom bus of,
74–75
tours of, 23, 24, 29–30, 44,
49–50, 54, 70
walks out on *Vogue* photo
shoot, 53–54
Franklin, Barbara Siggers
(mother), 17–18, 19–20, 94
sudden death of, 21
Franklin, Carolyn (sister), 17,
20, 38, 40, 41–42, 54, 64, 65,
66, 72
death of, 85
Franklin, Cecil (brother), 17, 19,
20, 24, 29, 47, 49, 59, 61, 66
death of, 85–86
Franklin, Clarence (son by
"Romeo"), 22, 49, 60, 62–63,
73
Franklin, Eddie (son by Edward),
25, 49, 60
Franklin, Erma (sister), 17, 20,

23, 25, 29, 30, 38, 63, 65, 66
Franklin, Kecalf (son by Ken E.
Cunningham), 49, 60
Franklin, Rachel (Big Mama)
(grandmother), 20, 21, 23, 29,
49
Franklin, Reverend Clarence
LaVaughn (C. L.) (father),
17–18, 22, 23, 25, 27, 48, 53
death of, 75
friendship with Martin Luther
King Jr., 24–25, 33–34
tragedy of, 62, 63, 66, 70
Franklin, Vaughn (brother), 17,
19, 29, 42, 86

G
Gaye, Marvin, 38, 75
Gaynor, Gloria, 58
Giant Step, 62
Gillespie, Dizzy, 34
Goodman, John, 12
Gordy, Berry, 19, 27, 31–32
Gospel, 18, 21, 22, 27, 48, 97
albums of Aretha Franklin,
52–53, 84–85
history of, 23–24
Gospel Caravan, 23, 24, 25
Gossett, Louis, Jr., 64
Goulet, Robert, 35
Grammy Awards, 12, 41, 53, 55,
60, 71, 78, 85, 87
Grier, Rosey, 62

H
Hamlisch, Marvin, 62
Hammond, John, 27–28, 29, 31
Harris, Teddy, 34–35
Hawkins, Roger, 39
Hill, Lauryn, 14, 96, 97
Holiday, Billie, 28, 45
Holley, Major, 27
Hollywood Squares, 60
Hooker, John Lee, 65
Hope, Bob, 60
Houston, Cissy, 39, 69

Houston, Whitney, 21, 39, 86,
99

I
Impressions, 59
International Creative
Management (ICM), 62

J
Jackson, Chuck, 57, 69
Jackson, Janet, 60
Jackson, Mahalia, 18, 21, 34, 74
death of, 52
Jackson, Michael, 60
Jackson, Reverend Jesse, 57, 70,
85, 93
Joel, Billy, 87
John, Elton, 86
Jones, Quincy, 54, 87

K
Kahn, Chaka, 58
Kennedy Center Honors, 94
King, Carole, 44, 53, 97
King, Jo, 27
King, Reverend Martin Luther,
Jr., 24–25, 33, 34, 51, 75
funeral of, 43–44
Knight, Gladys, 54

L
LaBelle, Patti, 29
Lady Soul. *See* Franklin, Aretha
Laugh-In, 40
Lennox, Annie, 78
Les Miserables, 88

M
McDonald, Michael, 88
Manchester, Melissa, 64
Mandela, Nelson, 87
Manilow, Barry, 64
Marden, Arif, 40, 53, 69, 70
Mayfield, Curtis, 59, 64
Mersey, Bob, 31
Michael, George, 82
Miller, Marcus, 71

Mills, Stephanie, 95
Miracles, 29
Moore, Lola, 21
Motown Records, 19, 27, 29, 31–32, 38, 47
MusiCares, 11, 13

N
Nathan, David, 57, 86
National Academy of Recording Arts and Sciences, 41, 53, 93
National Association for the Advancement of Colored People (NAACP), 71, 85
New Bethel Baptist Church (Detroit), 15, 18, 21, 22, 33, 63, 64, 75, 84, 86, 94, 95
New Breeders, 47
Newport Jazz Festival, 34
New Temple Missionary Baptist Church (Los Angeles), 52–53
New York Academy of Ballet, 61
New York Jazz Festival, 34

O
Oprah Winfrey Show, The, 95, 98–99
Otis, Clyde, 32

P
Pavarotti, Luciano, 11, 13
Phillips, Esther, 53
Pickett, Wilson, 37, 38
Presley, Elvis, 33, 39, 99
Preston, Billy, 95

Q
Queen of Soul. See Franklin, Aretha

R
Rawls, Lou, 93
Redding, Otis, 38, 40
Richards, Keith, 82

Robinson, Smokey, 19, 20, 29, 32, 48, 72
Rogers, Nile, 58
Rolling Stones, 31, 82
Ross, Diana, 19, 54

S
Sager, Carole Bayer, 62, 88
Sam & Dave, 38, 71
Shindig, 33
Simone, Nina, 52
Simpson, Valerie, 55
Sinatra, Frank, 48
Sinatra, Nancy, 41
Sing, Mahalia, Sing, 74
Sly and the Family Stone, 88
Smith, Bessie, 45
Smith, Liz, 94–95
Soulful Divas, The, 57
Soul Stirrers, 21, 22
Southern California Community Choir, 53
Southern Christian Leadership Conference, 43
Spann, Pervis, 42
Sparkle, 59, 60
Spinners, 64
Staples, Mavis, 85, 94
Staples Singers, 22
Stax Records, 38
Steely Dan, 69
Stewart, Jim, 38
Streisand, Barbra, 35, 48, 91
Summer, Donna, 58
Superfly, 59
Supremes, 19, 31, 59
Sweet Inspirations, 38–39, 42, 69

T
Temptations, 47
Tonight Show, The, 41, 60
Top of the Pops, 50

Turman, Glynn, 63–64, 66, 72, 73
Turner, Ike and Tina, 34

U
US Airways, 74

V
Vandross, Luther, 71, 72, 73, 89
Village People, 58

W
Walden, Narada Michael, 75–76, 82, 84, 88
Ward, Clara, 18, 21, 24, 54
Warhol, Andy, 82
Warwick, Dionne, 14, 44, 64–65, 72
Washington, Dinah, 31, 32, 34
Wells, Mary, 31, 32
Wexler, Jerry, 37, 40, 44, 50, 51, 52, 69
    discusses Aretha Franklin, 38, 39, 42–43
White, Ted, 30–31, 32, 39–40, 44, 45
White, Ted, Jr. (son by Ted White), 30–31, 49, 60, 70, 73
William Morris Agency, 64
Williams, Deniece, 72
Wilson, Jackie, 29, 75
Women of the Five Boroughs of New York, 58
Wonder, Stevie, 55, 64
Wood, Ron, 82

Y
Yancy, Marvin, 57
Young Rascals, 38
You Only Live Twice, 41

PICTURE CREDITS

JIM McAVOY, an alumnus of St. Joseph's University and currently an advertising professional, is also the author of *Tom Hanks* (Chelsea House, 2000) and *Mel Gibson* (Lucent, 2001). He lives and works near Philadelphia, Pennsylvania.

The author wishes to thank the following individuals for their help in the preparation of this work: Don McAvoy, Jarrod Cecere, Steven Clark at the Disney Channel, Dina Hossain at American Masters, Holly Drauglis at NARAS, and Rachel Lizerbram at VH1.